BARRY LYONS

Letter to a Prohibitionist

Barry Lyons has written on popular and classical music, and has contributed book reviews to *Prometheus*, a British quarterly devoted to the arts and sciences. *Letter to a Prohibitionist* is his first book.

Letter to a Prohibitionist

BARRY LYONS

Obladi Press
New York

THIRD OBLADI PRESS EDITION, JUNE 2011

lettertoaprohibitionist@gmail.com

ISBN: 1466388994
EAN-13: 978-1466388994

Cover design by Alison Paddock
www.zivartdesign.com

Printed in the United States of America

This letter is dedicated to William Bennett, Barry McCaffery, and John Walters, none of whom seem to know what the hell they're talking about.

I used to smoke marijuana. But I'll tell you something: I would only smoke it in the late evening. Oh, occasionally the early evening, but usually the late evening—or the mid-evening. Just the early evening, mid-evening and late evening. Occasionally, early afternoon, early mid-afternoon, or perhaps the late mid-afternoon. Oh, sometimes the early-mid-late-early morning but never at dusk. Never at dusk. I would never do that.

—Steve Martin

Letter to a Prohibitionist

First of all, I want to thank you for getting back to me. As I was writing my first letter—really, your op-ed against marijuana legalization was so wacky there was no way I could not respond, total stranger though you are to me—I was thinking I'd get no more than a few sentences out of you, if that, and yet here you are, catching me by surprise (though not off guard) with your hysterical squalling. And that conniption you had over my mentioning in passing that while we're at it we ought to take a look at the laws for other illicit drugs as well. Wow, I had no idea I was in favor of "legalizing drug abuse." That's fantastic. You've given me way more to work with. Thanks.

Where to begin? It's probably best to start with your closing comments, where you make clear your final thoughts on the matter. No need to pull out a copy of your letter. I have your summation typed out right here.

> The facts are these. Marijuana is as dangerous in its own way as any other illegal drug. The notion that it's a "recreational" substance is absurd in light of all the high drivers we'd have to contend with in your crazy world of legalized marijuana. And your claim that marijuana smoking has medical benefits is simply laughable on its face. No good can ever come from inhaling a bowl of burning plant matter.

Well, we can't both be right. You're either correct to say that marijuana is as dangerous as heroin—or alcohol, for that matter—or you are not; you're either correct to say that people with glaucoma or cerebral palsy who say that smoking marijuana reduces eye pressure and muscle tension are liars, or they are not; you're either correct to say that recreational marijuana smokers are a danger and a menace to us all, or you are not.

But as I reached the end of your letter you jolted me into remembering one of the more stunning facts one could ever cite about your ill-named "war on marijuana" (ill-named, because you can't wage war on a plant, you silly person; you can only wage war on people). It's not the realization that tens of billions of dollars have been lost to this decades-long debacle. It's not even the fact that hundreds of thousands of people since the dawn of this awful war have been arrested, charged, and jailed *for years* for the "crime" of having on their person a weed that grows wild in nature. No. It's the plain fact that this demented escapade of yours began two years *before Hitler invaded Poland.*

Now, you think you get off to a good start with that old chestnut about alcohol, that it has been "culturally sanctioned from time immemorial" and that "we" (society) don't need to "add" another drug to the marketplace of mind-altering substances. You tell me how booze "has long been woven into the fabric of daily life" but that marijuana is not so woven and that "we are rightly determined" it shall not become woven. Yes, booze is quite woven in our society, as one of this country's leading drug pushers, *The Wall Street Journal*, will attest. Not a week goes by without the paper extolling some vineyard or giving high praise to a cherished vintage. Hey, don't get me wrong. I like wine, and I think Jay McInerney's coverage for the *Journal* is a pleasure to read. I'm just saying.

But marijuana isn't some uninvited interloper who's crashed an alcohol-only party of your besotted imagining. Cannabis, the

Greek/Latin name for the plant that's also known as ganja (Sanskrit for "hemp," of which today we call the nonpsychoactive variety of cannabis), has been grown, harvested, and used congenially in many cultures for thousands of years. Fact is, and I do not use that phrase lightly, cannabis is one of the most beloved plants known to man.

Archaeologists are in general agreement that the plant was first cultivated at least six thousand years ago and perhaps even further back—and it's quite possible that cannabis may have been the *first* plant we turned to for all sorts of reasons conducive to our well being. We not only ate the seeds of the plant, we also made clothing and rope from its fibers. An ancient Chinese burial site dating back to the Zhou dynasty (1046–256 B.C.) was discovered in 1972, and fragments of cloth made of hemp were found, making it one of the oldest preserved specimens of hemp in existence. We also have evidence that hemp was used in ancient Japan and India.

As for the United States, it must drive you batshit to be reminded that hemp was a prized commodity in the early years of this country. Sorry, but you're just going to have to accept this fact of history—and the words of some Founding Fathers. "Hemp is of first necessity to the wealth & protection of the country," said Thomas Jefferson, and he put that sentiment in writing: he drafted the Declaration of Independence on hemp paper, thanks to Benjamin Franklin, whose first paper mill produced paper made from hemp. More: "Make the most you can of the Indian Hemp seed and sow it everywhere"—George Washington; "We shall, by and by, want a world of hemp more for our own consumption"—John Adams.

And long before those fathers did their founding, a law was passed in 1619 in the colony of Jamestown *ordering* farmers to grow hemp. Yes, we were down with cannabis in a big way: we were smoking it (though, admittedly, not until around the mid-nineteenth century), eating it, and wearing it *long* before you and your kind began creating trouble for the rest of us. I'm talking about *way* back. Check this out.

"The world's earliest known marijuana smoker was a fourteen-year-old girl who apparently died 1,600 years ago while giving birth. THC [tetrahydrocannabinol, the psychoactive ingredient in marijuana] was found in the abdominal area of her skeletal remains in a tomb near Jerusalem." Hmm. Was marijuana used as an aid to lessen the pain of birth? We can only speculate. But one thing's for sure. Marijuana didn't kill this woman. We can say this with confidence, because no one, and I mean no one, in the history of the world has ever died from consuming marijuana.* And good news for women: where pregnancy is concerned, there is no cannabis equivalent for fetal alcohol syndrome.

So, okay, finding traces of marijuana among skeletal remains is pretty neat. But wouldn't it be way cooler to find an ancient dime bag? Here you go. Several years ago the world's oldest stash was discovered in a tomb in China that dates back to—hold on to your bong—700 B.C. You have to ask yourself, what kind of knucklehead would leave behind some primo weed with a goddamn corpse? It's not a mystery as to why: to get high in the afterlife. Yes, with the arrival of religion (when has it not been with us), shamans and the like concluded that the "trance"-inducing qualities of certain plants (and not just pot) were gifts from the gods.

But before early man used cannabis in a ritualistic fashion of whatever stripe, we had to experience that first inhalation of marijuana smoke. No one can know for sure but it's reasonable to assume that our first intake

*Prescription drugs kill at least twenty-five thousand people per year because of wrong dosage, incorrect use, or because of some out-of-the-blue adverse reaction. Marijuana? We're still waiting for a user to show up at the morgue, dead from pot.

of weed probably occurred at a campfire for cooking or perhaps at a fire at the mouth of a cave to keep away animals at night. This speculation is fine as far as it goes, but let's take this back even further. We had to first discover that we specifically *liked* inhaling marijuana and not maple leaves before assigning any ritualistic function to the plant. In other words, we had to first sort the good (desired) plants from the bad (noxious). If this sounds like evolution talk, you're right.

Here's the thing with Darwin and why this is important. You're on record, videotape actually, for saying marijuana growers "cultivate poison." A brainectomy might be in order here, but I'd rather you recognize your crazy talk for what it is. If marijuana were truly poisonous, we would have learned long ago to stay away from the plant just as we've learned to not consume azaleas. To put this in the language of natural selection, if cannabis were a poison, we would've selected the plant out of our daily lives thousands of generations ago. Or as *The Onion* put it satirically in one of their headlines, "Deaths of 550,000 Confirm Which Mushrooms Are Okay To Eat." Perfect.

So going back to our corpse with the weed, not only did we *not* remove marijuana from our daily experience in a world where we had supernatural "explanations" for nearly everything, with some no doubt amplified by the imaginative "visions" produced by pot, we made sure that certain shamans and dignitaries were *buried* with it. You see where I'm going with this. In case you don't, look at poison ivy.

Most of us do a pretty good job in our summery shorts of staying away from this plant lest we develop itchy and oozing pustules a few days later. How is it that we can do this? We recognize the leaves. This is a classic example of Darwinian natural selection in action: we literally avoid poison ivy (as best we can). We remove it—select it out—from our environment. We don't eat it, we don't smoke it, and we certainly won't walk barelegged through a patch of the stuff. Poison ivy, for those of us who are allergic to it, is *planta non grata* in our lives.

Consider an ad from those chowderheads at The Partnership for a Drug-Free America. We see an opened book. On the left-hand side there's a leaf labeled "Poison Ivy." On the right is another leaf labeled "Marijuana." The first sentence we read is: "Why is it parents can explain the harmful effects of one and not the other?" Because pot-smoking boomers know it's bullshit to equate pleasurable pot with miserable poison ivy. I have a message for the folks who conceived this particular spot: this is your brain on drug-war mendacities. Any questions?

As for *your* mendacities, I've caught you on many occasions sounding like a kindred spirit to the drug warriors from the Spanish Inquisition, and while nobody expects the Spanish Inquisition, in your case it's apt. Consider this wacky piece of wingnuttery, a snippet by the supremo drug warrior of that time—the Catholic Church:

> Inasmuch as the use of the herb or root called peyote has been introduced into [Mexico] for the purposes of detecting thefts, or divining other happenings, and of foretelling future events, it is an act of superstition condemned as opposed to the purity and integrity of our Holy Catholic Faith [and that all] mental images, fantasies and hallucinations [brought on by this substance] are plainly the suggestion and intervention of the Devil, the real author of this vice…

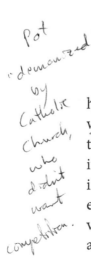

Cannabis was also used by "pagan herbalists" and was soon associated with witches, who were consequently viewed as a threat to Rome. See, the Catholic Church saw itself as the only source for performing healings, and as for cannabis, whose virtues were extolled by the Benedictine abbess Hildegard von Bingen—it "diminishes the bad humours and makes the good humours strong"—the church saw it and any other outside source of healing (and worship: can-nabis was used in "satanic masses") as threats to the "one true faith." Pope Innocent VIII eventually issued a papal bull condemning all hallucinogenic herbs. Where drug taking was once a way to commune with the gods it was now a way to dance with the devil. This change of heart is one that we cling to in decadent form to this day. After all, just look at yourself. The inquisitor's tone is hardly that removed from your fulminations on marijuana, which, to quote you, "obliterates morals, devalues character, our relations with each other, and our relation to God."

But as a secularist who is ill-suited for toiling in the fields of biblical exegesis, I must confess, as it were, that I'm confused by your insinuation that the Big One in the sky is a discriminating botanist who sorts "good" drugs from "bad." How it happens that Mother Nature could see to it that negative moral attributes inhere in certain ingestibles but not in others remains a cosmic mystery unexplained by you and your saintly brethren. But admit it, you must feel a wee bit of camaraderie with the writer of that peyote condemnation. True, many who dared question the authority of the church during the Inquisition were subjected to fiery deaths, and while you have "asked" us to get with the pogrom, you have deigned to not emulate Torquemada and for that we are most grateful.

But dude, I have some shocking news for you: the Bible was written by stoners. "Kaneh bosm" and "kannabus," obvious derivatives of the word "cannabis," appear several times throughout the Hebrew text. Revelation 22:1–2 ends with "...and the leaves of the tree were for the healing of the nations." Yeah? I'll bet you they weren't talking about jojoba (and it seems your buddy Jesus in the NT probably used cannabis oil to help the near-blind see. Good going, J-man). But of all the passages that can be construed as references to cannabis—"calamus" in the Song of Solomon is another (though the translation remains in dispute)—my favorite remains this alluring little passage, from Ezekiel I: "Spread out above the heads of the living creatures was what looked like an expanse, sparkling like ice, and awesome." I'll have a hit of that.

FAST FORWARD to the early twentieth century and we see religious agitation receding (only somewhat) in favor of secular condemnation, particularly with the rise of "yellow journalism"—sensationalist news stories coupled with outright lies and rumormongering—that depicted blacks and Mexicans as "frenzied beasts," with black musicians coming in for special scorn because of their "devil's music." We can thank newspaper magnate William Randolph Hearst for this development.

Once upon a time Hearst was friendly with Porfirio Díaz, the Mexican dictator, but this relationship soured when some of Pancho Villa's goons looted his ranch, Babicora, during the Mexican Revolution of 1910–1920. It would be fair to say that this event did not endear him to the locals, and in no time flat Hearst began publishing stories about loathsome Mexicans streaming over the border with their "loco" weed.

But one alternative narrative has it that Hearst was more concerned about hemp because as a source for making paper, he saw it as a threat to his timber interests. And so the plant had to go. Congress was petitioned, they took up the cause, and gave us the 1937 Marihuana Tax Act (that's the Mexican Spanish spelling of the word), which, it should be noted, didn't exactly criminalize anything. The government simply stated with this law that in order to grow cannabis you had to get some tax stamps from the government—but with a catch: they weren't giving stamps out to anybody.* You can't say the government doesn't have a sly sense of humor. So while the Act didn't make the possession and use of marijuana against the law (outright prohibition would happen later), it did amount to de facto prohibition. As for Hearst, it is believed by many that he explicitly supported the Act through some backdoor talks. If only history were that easy.

In his authoritative biography, W. A. Swanberg tells us that Hearst almost lost his shirt to Canadian paper producers because of massive debts incurred by price hikes. Hearst was using newsprint by the "thousands of tons," and where he was once paying about forty dollars per ton, by the late 1930s "the price of newsprint rose to forty-five dollars, to fifty and higher, costing the Hearst chain alone an extra five million dollars a year." So did Hearst, a businessman presumably after a solid bottom line as any talk up the virtues of hemp, which would have saved him tons of money? No, and as a way to save his ass he hawked his art collection. Question: if an expensive reliance on tree-based paper was the cause of his going broke, why would he hawk his art collection to scrape up cash

*An exemption was made for purchasers of birdseed on the grounds that if our avian friends did not consume hemp seeds they would not "sing sweetly." So birds could get a buzz on, but human beings could not. I see.

when instead he could have turned to cheap and easy-to-grow hemp?

So to Hearst-killed-hemp conspirators everywhere, I'm sorry to report that marijuana prohibition truly is rooted in racism, plain and simple. In fact, it wouldn't be far-fetched at all to say that the seeds of marijuana prohibition took root as an offshoot of "Manifest Destiny," the inchoate notion (it was never a formal policy) that the United States was divinely ordained—for white folk, you see. One way to remove "undesirables" from conquered territories was to hatch a drug war, and so it came to pass: opium, widely used among the Chinese, was outlawed in San Francisco in 1875, making it the first U.S. anti-drug law. Not long after, "Mexican opium"—marijuana—became a target for prohibition.

You could say that this quest for purity functioned as a two-track campaign, one against alcohol (the greater concern of up-tight pricks everywhere as we approached the 1920s), and the other against marijuana. As the prohibitionists demonized "whiskey-sodden Micks, wine-soaked wops, traitorous beer-swilling Krauts and liquor-selling Jew shopkeepers," it was very easy to tack on, almost as an afterthought, a campaign to go after blacks and Mexicans, the two groups of people who were most associated with smoking marijuana. "I wish I could show you what a small marijuana cigarette can do to one of our degenerate Spanish-speaking residents," it was said at the hearings for the Tax Act. And with such cheery sentiments echoing across the land in the halls of congress and in the tabloids, the campaign against marijuana was born.

To get you up to speed on the general tenor of the time, here's an exciting item from *The San Francisco Examiner* (a Hearst newspaper!), in 1923: "Marihuana Makes Fiends of Boys in Thirty Days." Do tell.

> "By the tons it is coming into this country—the deadly, dreadful poison that racks and tears not only the body, but the very heart and soul of every human being who once becomes a slave to it.... Marihuana is a short cut to the insane asylum. Smoke marihuana cigarettes for a month and what was once your brain will be nothing but a storehouse of horrid specters [and] makes a murderer who kills for the love of killing out of the mildest mannered man who ever laughed at the idea that any habit could ever get him."

Offering accompaniment a decade later, in 1934, *The Journal of American Nursing* tells us that anyone who smokes marijuana "will suddenly turn with murderous violence upon whomever is nearest to him. He will run amuck with knife, axe, gun, or anything else that is close at hand, and will kill or maim without any reason." Well, there's certainly a horrid specter of murderous violence going on among drug *gangs*, but last I looked, all seems to be peace and quiet among lovey-dovey marijuana *smokers*, with Pink Floyd streaming through the headphones.*

But as you look back at your forebears, whom do you turn to for intellectual sustenance? If studying the cosmos were your bag, you might say Galileo. If you were interested in evolution, you'd say Darwin. Physics, Einstein. So who is it for you? Permit me to make a nomination. I don't think this is bold of me. I mean, really, the choice is pretty obvious, isn't it? *The* founding father of marijuana prohibition is none other than Harry J. Anslinger.

Wow, what an inspiring life he led. First, he worked in the Bureau of Prohibition, and then when that gig was nixed by the repeal of the Eighteenth Amendment, he went on to serve in the Treasury Department's Federal Bureau of Narcotics for thirty-two years. From pursuing alcohol makers to hunting

*Somewhere in the world right now a barroom brawl is breaking out and yet I remain hard pressed to think of the last time I heard of a fight among friends who were getting high. Hollywood has given us *The Big Lebowski*, but we've never seen a story about a violent and angry stoner. Want to know why? Nobody would believe it.

down marijuana users. Way to go, Ans. Was that a lateral move or a promotion? Let's now consider some of this thoughtful man's remarks on the subject of menacing marijuana.

> How many murders, suicides, robberies, criminal assaults, hold-ups, burglaries, and deeds of maniacal insanity [marijuana] causes each year, especially among the young can only be conjectured. [Can only be *imagined* is more accurate.]

> The primary reason to outlaw marijuana is its effect on the degenerate races.

> There are 100,000 total marijuana smokers in the US, and most are Negroes, Hispanics, Filipinos and entertainers. Their satanic music, jazz and swing, result from marijuana usage. This marijuana causes white women to seek sexual relations with Negroes, entertainers and any others.

> Colored students at the University of Minnesota partying with [white] female students, smoking [marijuana] and getting their sympathy with stories of racial persecution. Result: pregnancy.

This is stirring stuff. Of course, humble me, I'm in no position to measure the strong affection you must have for this man. Do get back to me with an encomium.

Pop music also chimed in during Anslinger's day. Consider these rollicking lines from "Smokin' Reefer," from 1932: "It's the kind of stuff that dreams are made of/It's the thing that white folks are afraid of." Turning to flickering celluloid, the biggest hit—well, not until it played as a hoot on the college circuit in the 1970s—is *Reefer Madness*, the reigning champ of kooky propaganda. Why hasn't this film been brought up to date? I'd like to see some terrifying depictions of pot-fueled cancer victims, nauseated by chemotherapy, wreaking havoc with guns and knives on nurses, friends, and family.*

And now for some sobering news. While Anslinger and his goons—excuse me, associates—were getting all apoplectic about pot, some studies at the time, with a few even predating Anslinger, were coming to different conclusions about weed.

IN 1893, THE INDIA Hemp Drugs Commission examined cannabis use in India. The study showed that medicinal and recreational use of the plant was not deleterious to the inhabitants—and so the British Crown saw no reason to criminalize the plant. Next.

---

*In the years leading up to marijuana prohibition, the plant was condemned because it made users violent and crazy. In the late 1940s, the government changed its tune: marijuana was condemned not because it turned people into murderous maniacs, no sir, but because it turned people into Communist-loving pacifists.

In 1925 the governor of the Panama Canal Zone asked for an official inquiry on the alleged hazards of marijuana use. And what conclusions were made? The committee recommended "that no steps be taken by the Canal Zone authorities to prevent the sale or use of marijuana, and that no special legislation be asked for." Next.

Fiorello La Guardia, as mayor of New York City, spearheaded an investigation into the dangers of marijuana. He discovered, upon release of a report in 1944, that "marijuana is not the determining factor in the commission of major crimes" and that "the publicity concerning the catastrophic effects of marijuana smoking in New York City is unfounded." This infuriated Anslinger, who soon turned to "degenerate Hollywood" to make his case, with the colorful arrest and imprisonment of Robert Mitchum on a marijuana possession charge serving as the highlight of that endeavor. In early 1949, the actor got forty-three days at a prison farm.

In 1972, *The Consumers Union Report of Licit and Illicit Drugs* gave us reason to believe that common sense was about to prevail: "Consumers Union recommends the immediate repeal of all federal laws governing the growing, processing, transportation, sale, possession, and uses of marijuana" and that "each of the fifty states similarly repeal its existing marijuana laws and pass new laws legalizing the cultivation, processing, and orderly marketing of marijuana—subject to appropriate regulations." If only these observations were the last word on the subject. It was not to be because of the arrival of a new menace on the scene: the thirty-seventh President of the United States. Here we go, from the morning of May 26, 1971.

> Richard Nixon: "Now, this is one thing I want. I want a goddamn strong statement on marijuana. Can I get that out of this sonofabitching, uh, Domestic Council?"
> H.R. Haldeman: "Sure."
> RN: "I mean one on marijuana that just tears the ass out of them. I see another thing in the news summary this morning about it. You know it's a funny thing, every one of the bastards that are out for legalizing marijuana is Jewish. What the Christ is the matter with the Jews, Bob, what is the matter with them? I suppose it's because most of them are psychiatrists, you know, there's so many, all the greatest psychiatrists are Jewish. By God we are going to hit the marijuana thing, and I want to hit it right square in the puss, I want to find a way of putting more on that. More [unintelligible] work with somebody else with this."
> HRH: "Mm hmm, yep."
> RN: "I want to hit it, against legalizing and all that sort of thing."

Ah, yes, a prime example of marijuana inducing paranoia in a person who has never used it. And so Nixon created The National Commission on Marijuana and Drug Abuse, now generally referred to as The Shafer Commission, so-named, because of Raymond P. Shafer, a former governor of Pennsylvania, who headed up the investigation. The committee's conclusions? "[T]he criminal law is too harsh a tool to apply to personal possession even in the effort to discourage use. It implies an overwhelming indictment of the behavior, which we believe is not appropriate. The actual and potential harm of use of the drug is not great enough to justify intrusion by the criminal law into private behavior, a step which our society takes only with the greatest reluctance." And this: "Marijuana's relative potential for harm to the vast majority of individual users and its actual impact on society does not justify a social policy designed to seek out and firmly punish those who use it."

Days before the report was released Nixon got wind of it and assailed the committee members as a "bunch of do-gooders" and "soft on marijuana." He had a solution. "We need, and I use the word 'all out war,' on all fronts. We have to attack on all fronts." And so with that fine up yours to the committee and his pent-up desire to tear the ass out of the nation, Nixon launched the "modern" war on marijuana. A splendid time was not guaranteed for all, particularly for those who happened to not have pale skin, as the numbers have repeatedly shown, even to this day, that whites have always been in the minority when it comes to the persecution of marijuana smokers.

A few years later, President Carter attempted to bring some sense to the issue. Here he is, on August 2, 1977: "Penalties against drug use should not be more damaging to an individual than the use of the drug itself. Nowhere is this more clear than in the laws against the possession of marijuana in private for personal use. Therefore, I support legislation amending Federal law to eliminate all Federal criminal penalties for the possession of up to one ounce of marijuana." We know how that turned out.

Well, then, Ronald Reagan to the rescue? "I now have absolute proof that smoking even one marijuana cigarette is equal in brain damage to being on Bikini Island during an H-bomb blast." Hmm. So vaporizing cannabis is on par with vaporizing citizens of Hiroshima and Nagasaki. I'll have to look into that.

And then we move on to George Bush Sr., who brought an end to the Compassionate Investigational New Drug Study in 1992, a program devised by the government to dispense marijuana to a limited number of individuals for medical reasons (more on that in a bit), and Bill Clinton who did nothing for the cause except to intensify the war on pot smokers during his tenure. Perhaps if Clinton had inhaled he might've taken a different view. But it's possible he's inhaled since then. In December 2000, only weeks before walking out of the Oval Office for the last time, he told a *Rolling Stone* reporter that he supported the growing decriminalization movement. That's swell of him. I guess his having considered the four million people arrested on marijuana charges, arrests that he oversaw as Commander-in Chief, belatedly stirred his conscience.

And yet you counter with the argument that marijuana smokers *are* worthy of arrest because they are doing something that is prohibited. Well, yes. Marijuana smokers certainly break laws, but I'm at a loss to see what *crimes* these folks commit. I mean, in a continuum of crimes, from the petty (stealing candy from a drugstore) to the severe (sending anthrax in the mail), I'm hard pressed to figure out where marijuana smoking would be pegged. Really, inhaling marijuana just isn't on par with losing money in a pyramid scheme or having your livelihood as a fisherman destroyed by the criminal negligence of an oil company.

I'm going to hazard a guess here and say that you are suffering from an acute case of drug-law euphoria. Really, the fog of a hearty marijuana exhalation has got to be clearer than any of your exhortations on the subject. You've bleated many startling things over the years, but this first one is particularly alarming:

> The battle [for a winnable war] primarily will be one of the mind—for the constraints that have to be accepted by a progressive and free society. Americans need to know the truth about our common enemy and must be encouraged, as they were during the great wars, by the same unambiguous media that helped the nation to victory.

To have liberty we must remove liberty. We must destroy the village in order to save it. The media, that the Constitution means to maintain as an open market of opinion, must be "unambiguous." That dagger you just plunged into the heart of the Constitution. Is it smooth or serrated?

> If we take this approach to every problem that poses difficulty to the criminal justice

> system, then we should no longer penalize breaking and entering, since we only solve between eight and fourteen percent of all housebreaks.
>
> A lot of people don't obey the highway speed limit, so why not repeal all speeding laws?
>
> By this logic, armed robbery should be legalized.
>
> The government must not negotiate with the underworld. This leads only to unacceptable compromises.
>
> Drug dealers should be subjected to the same sentences imposed on murderers.

Whoa, that last one is intense. Surely you ought to be holding all tobacco and liquor store "dealers" responsible for infinitely more murder. But I particularly like your one about negotiating with the underworld. This has the contours of classic farce—except that nobody is laughing: create the underworld with prohibition laws, and then complain about "unacceptable compromises" with the criminal class *you* created. But to speak of *true* criminal behavior is to speak of *real* victims. What's a real victim? Well, that's easy: when an armed robbery occurs we have an aggressor—the guy with the gun—and the aggrieved, victimized party: the storeowner emptying his cash register. Or, when someone breaks into a house… You get the picture—but you don't, which is why it's embarrassing to have to explain to you some basic ethical precepts that even a nine-year-old is equipped to understand.

As for the supposed crime of marijuana smoking, I've always noticed that pot smokers never seem to want to complain about a crime for which they don't feel victimized.* There's a simple explanation for this: because these people *choose* to smoke marijuana, they don't feel victimized when they decide to spark up a joint and inhale its contents. But, hey, you want a real victim? Donald Scott thought he was living lawfully in his California home when he was subjected to a dawn raid instigated by a drug-law-addicted DEA official who adventitiously flew over the man's property the previous evening and saw what he thought were marijuana plants. Scott was shot dead and no marijuana plants were found.

And then there's Mildred Kaitz, a seventy-nine-year-old mother in New York who was arrested for growing marijuana for her son, who was suffering from multiple sclerosis. She said the police officers asked her,

---

*Though I can think of three ways in which one can be a victim of *prohibition*: you bought some schwag you can't return, you got killed by some thug, or you got arrested for possession or selling.

"What if your son needed an operation? Would you rob a bank?" Although she said she would, what's more disturbing is the nature of the question, the insinuation that growing a plant *on her property* and peacefully harvesting its fruit is somehow not an inalienable right.

Here's what you need to know, and consider this a gratis refresher course in the Fourth Amendment: "The right of the people to be secure in their persons, houses, papers, and effects, against unreasonable searches and seizures, shall not be violated, and no Warrants shall issue, but upon probable cause, supported by Oath or affirmation, and particularly describing the place to be searched, and the persons or things to be seized."

I think it's fair to say that pot smokers who aren't bothering anybody aren't secure in their persons, including the non-smoker Ms. Kaitz—I guess she ought to be regarded as an in-house trafficker, delivering pot to her son directly from the garden—who was given probation and told to "keep out of trouble" if she wanted to have the marijuana conviction erased from her record—a record, mind you, she never had until she was arrested for no good reason at all.

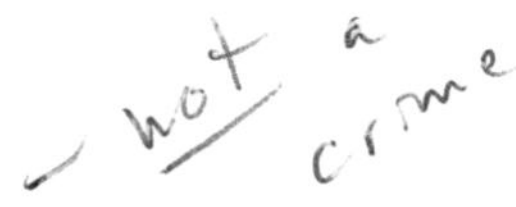

I WANT TO GET across to you in no uncertain terms that the "crime" of marijuana possession or growing or smoking or transporting is no crime at all but an offense that exists only in your imagination. By the same token, you can't make cannabis illegal any more than you can make sand or seagulls illegal. Nature is nature. It exists apart from human morality.* It can't be criminalized.

What's worse, you bring new meaning to the phrase "crime against nature," which is your refusal to accept the reality of a particular fundamental human drive. First, what are some fundamental human drives? I can think of four: to seek water to quench thirst, food to kill hunger, protection from the elements, and downtime to facilitate sleep. And sex. That's about it, right? Nope. You missed a sixth category: the desire to alter one's state of consciousness. Hey, even a child who's playing wants to have this experience every now and then. See that little tyke over there twirling around and around until he falls to the ground? There you go: evidence that our desire to engage in mind-altering activities begins when we are kids. So it's time you face a simple truth that spans all generations, continents, and the history of

*"Drugs are evil" is a favorite leitmotif of yours. Two questions: *how* is this possible? And how long have you felt this way about alcohol?

humankind: *all* of us like to get high doing *some*thing, and a good many of us do so by ingesting certain types of vegetation (or synthetic drugs, as the case may be). I'll let the integrative medicine specialist Andrew Weil sum this up. These experiences (of getting high) "are vital to us because they are expressions of our unconscious minds, and the integration of conscious and unconscious experience is the key to life, health, and spiritual development."

You know what though? You remind me of James Randi. Thing is, I like James Randi. He's done us a great service over the years exposing all sorts of pseudoscience for the flimflammery junk that it is. But take a look at what the famed psychic-phenomena debunker once had to say about recreational drugs:

> I want to be as sure of the world, the real world, around me as is possible. Now, you can only attain that to a certain degree, but I want the greatest degree of control. I've never involved myself in narcotics of any kind; I don't smoke, I don't drink because that can easily fuzz the edges of my rationality, fuzz the edges of my reasoning powers and I want to be as aware as I possibly can. That means giving up a lot of fantasies that might be comforting in some ways, but I'm willing to give that up in order to live in an actually real world, as close as I can get to it.

His use of "fantasies" is a bit off the mark here. The buzz we get from alcohol isn't a fantasy as such; it's simply an alternate state of mind that drinkers find pleasurable. But I don't begrudge Randi's general view. If he never wants to bring on a drug-induced altered state of mind, fine. More power to him if that's how he feels. But guess what? We can point to another individual in a related field who held the precise opposite view.

Some years back, Daffy's, the clothing chain, had an ad that mocked their pricier competitors: "No wonder they call it high fashion. To dream up some of those prices you'd have to be high." This is nothing more than a silly variant of "he must be smoking something," the insinuation that to be high on marijuana is to live in netherworld of mental disarray. Try telling that to Carl Sagan (I wish we could; he'd get a good laugh out of it). Here he is, talking about pot:

> When I'm high I can penetrate into the past, recall childhood memories, friends, relatives, playthings, streets, smells, sounds, and tastes from a vanished era. I can reconstruct the actual occurrences in childhood events only half understood at the time. Many but not all my cannabis trips have somewhere in them a symbolism significant to me which I won't attempt to describe here, a kind of mandala embossed on the high. Free-associating to this mandala, both visually and as plays on

> words, has produced a very rich array of insights. There is a myth about such highs: the user has an illusion of great insight, but it does not survive scrutiny in the morning. I am convinced that this is an error, and that the devastating insights achieved when high are real insights; the main problem is putting these insights in a form acceptable to the quite different self that we are when we're down the next day. Some of the hardest work I've ever done has been to put such insights down on tape or in writing. The problem is that ten, even more, interesting ideas or images have to be lost in the effort of recording one. … The illegality of cannabis is outrageous, an impediment to full utilization of a drug which helps produce the serenity and insight, sensitivity, and fellowship so desperately needed in this increasingly mad and dangerous world.

Yes, marijuana smoking does lead to good ideas, many of which, as Sagan noted, often seem to coming tripping, as it were, over each other. I believe I speak for many when I say that where alcohol tends to bring on a lethargic, molasses-laden heaviness of mind,* marijuana, when it doesn't make you sleepy (depends on what you're smoking), tends to stimulate thought and make the user feel mentally nimble—though, sure, virtually

---

*And alcohol often tends to bring out or amplify aggressiveness in some drinkers. Hey, trust me, you'd rather be trapped in an elevator with a bunch of stoners than with a bunch of drunks.

any evening spent getting high with a friend will have at least one "What was I just talking about?" uttered before the night is over.

Okay, so Sagan and Weil maintain that marijuana enhances the life of the mind (and I'll have lots more to say about this in a bit). No disagreement there. But what about physical health? One peeve of yours you find worth petting is the idea that legalized marijuana would be a major health drag on society. Consider this *Reuters* news item and particularly my added italics for emphasis: "An estimated one hundred and sixty-six million people worldwide have either tried using cannabis or are active users of the drug *despite scientific research showing its adverse effects on health...*" Adverse effects on health? *What* adverse effects on health? Apart from possible cases of bronchitis for the most consistent and dedicated of pot smokers (a problem easily rectified if one vaporizes), essentially zero ill effect is associated with marijuana.

Here's a fact that should blow your mind: cannabinoids exist in the plant, and corresponding receptors for "receiving" those cannabinoids exist in our brains. The very existence of these receptors in our noggins would suggest that it isn't far-fetched at all (this hasn't been confirmed) to say that our evolutions—the growth of the plant; the growth of our brains—were possibly intertwined. You might even say we are one with the plant. But what are cannabinoids you ask? Bear with me. I promise this won't take long.

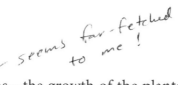

Cannabinoids are a group of compounds found in cannabis that also occur naturally in our nervous and immune systems. Further, cannabinoids are structurally related to THC and bind to what we refer to in the brain as cannabinoid receptors. It's been reasoned that there had to be a highway, if you will, between the marijuana cannabinoids—the THC in the plant—and the receptors in the brain that enable us to experience the high. Thing is, there are roughly fifty or so cannabinoids in marijuana and so we don't really know which ones are doing the trick (giving us the high), which ones that modify the high, and which ones that don't do shit.

Now, the matching receptors in the brain that we all assumed had to be there were discovered in the 1980s, and favorable-to-pot neurotransmitters were found in the lower brain *and* in the hippocampus. What is the hippocampus? Put simply, it is the locus of memory and the arena of the brain most associated with our creative nature. This goes far in explaining why some writers and many musicians turn to pot to get those free-association juices flowing.* But you're not buying it. You insist that all pot smokers are slackers.

"The problem with all of the arguments favoring legalization of marijuana use," you write, "is that the rest of us, nonusers who can keep a job and pay taxes, will be feeding and housing these losers forever." Hmm. All men are mortal; Socrates is a man; therefore, Socrates is mortal. If marijuana is a substance that leads irrevocably to amotivation and slackerdom, it ought to amotivate and slackerize anyone who uses it. So what accounts for these anomalistic, motivated marijuana users like Carl Sagan? Better question: *was* Sagan an anomaly or was he just one successful marijuana smoker among many? You claim that "[marijuana] is a one-way ticket to dead-end hopes and dreams." Oh yeah? Let's do a brief roll call of some celebrity losers and dead-enders who saw their hopes and dreams dashed and destroyed by marijuana.

Richard Branson, founder of Virgin Group is, in your view, a loser. Bill Gates, listed by *Forbes* as one of the top three richest men in the world, is also a loser. Ted Turner, founder of CNN, is another major burnout.

---

*Which is exactly what Lady Gaga was insinuating in her *60 Minutes* interview with Anderson Cooper: "I smoke a lot of pot when I write music." As an artist who knows how pot can spark the imagination, she's hardly alone (more examples coming up on the next page).

Turning to the world of entertainment, Bill Maher, long-time pot smoker and funny man, who hosts his own successful HBO show, is a loser. If we are to believe an ex-wife of his, Tony Bennett, who is regarded by many as the greatest living exponent of the Great American Songbook, is said to have spent a good part of the 1970s stoned. Therefore, by your lights, Bennett is a loser. Another successful loser, Wanda Sykes, was asked by Jay Leno how making more money has changed her life. She said she could now buy better weed. Willie Nelson, one of the most successful songwriters around, is a loser. And going a bit further back into the history of music, let's not forget one of the most famous losers of all time, that trumpeter and singer who managed to maintain a successful career for decades. Yes, I'm speaking of Louis Armstrong. And then we have Thelonious Monk, Lester Young, The Beatles, Bob Dylan, Keith Richards (who taught Richard Branson how to roll a joint)... Gee, are there any musicians out there who *haven't* smoked pot?

Although many celebrity stoners are not shy about their pot use—verbally, that is—the award for the Most Audacious Behavior in a Public Setting, given out posthumously, I'm sorry to say, goes to Robert Altman, who, in 2001, lit up a joint at table "with" the Prime Minister of the United Kingdom of Great Britain and Northern Ireland. Sorry, Tony. You can look the other way but you can't smell the other way. There's no way Blair was not aware of what was going on—and yet no one proceeded to tap Mr. Altman on the shoulder to kindly remind the great director that cannabis smoking was not permitted in front of the prime minister. With Jerry Hall, Dave Stewart, and other luminaries sitting nearby, it must have been a fun evening. Everyone's getting baked—except Tony Blair, who no doubt wished for someone to pass him the joint.

And then there's Michael Phelps. The man is not a dope, but he is a wimp. Take a look at his statement that was released within days of that photo hitting the Web, you know, the one with him taking a hit off a bong.

> I engaged in behavior which was regrettable and demonstrated bad judgment. I'm twenty-three years old, and despite the successes I've had in the pool, I acted in a youthful and inappropriate way, not in a manner people have come to expect from me. For this, I am sorry. I promise my fans and the public it will not happen again.

Not long after, the International Olympic Committee released a statement in response:

"Michael Phelps is a great Olympic champion. He apologized for his inappropriate behavior. We have no reason to doubt his sincerity and his commitment to continue to act as a role model." Let me dissect this.

"Michael Phelps is a great Olympic champion." Agreed. "He apologized for his inappropriate behavior." Yes, he did. The mystery is why he apologized. When considering the context in which he sucked back on a bong—at a *party* (and not in competition or training mode)—I fail to see what was inappropriate about his behavior. "We have no reason to doubt his sincerity and his commitment to continue to act as a role model." Role model? I thought Phelps was a swimmer. But I don't for a second doubt Phelps's sincere intentions at that party: he grabbed the bong when it was handed to him and inhaled its contents. For all I care he could have chugged back a can of Budweiser.

And then we have Ross Rebagliati, the Canadian snowboarder, who temporarily lost his gold medal because of a pot charge. Temporarily? Yes. Rebagliati's medal was returned, because it was decided that he committed no wrongdoing vis-à-vis the Olympics rules: marijuana is not a performance-enhancing drug. No kidding. Neither is beer.

But forget about celebrities. What about the rest of us? Here is the news: stoners live among us. See that woman on the train over there who's got you all googly eyes? She's a "stiletto stoner."

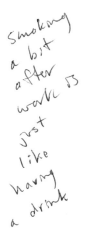

"I hate the term *pothead*—it connotes that I'm high 24/7, which I'm not," said one woman, in a *Marie Claire* piece on female stoners. "I don't need it to get through my day. I just enjoy it when my day is over." Said another about her evening indulgence: "It's my moment for myself before I have to get up and do it all over again tomorrow. It's my bubble bath." Another: "I have a stressful job. I have a baby. I need to unwind somehow, and I don't really like to drink." I like this one:

> I'm a middle-aged woman, college educated and married over twenty years to a public servant (who doesn't indulge) and we have two teenage kids. I volunteer for a host of community organizations, attend lots of local youth athletic events, and by all accounts I'm an engaged community member. By day I run a local non-profit, but on the occasional Friday night after a long and tiresome work week, and only when the kids aren't home, I go in the bathroom, open the window a crack, and mom lights up a little pink, sparkly pipe and smokes the ganja, falling into the most blissful, relaxed state ever.

But here's something else you need to know about these stiletto stoners and other nine-to-five office workers of both sexes who happen to smoke pot. They hold down their jobs in exactly the same way most alcohol drinkers do—which takes me to drug testing.

If we don't test capable and responsible individuals for alcohol use—and use, mind you, that occurs during off hours—then there's no need to test these people for marijuana use. Besides, marijuana metabolites tell us nothing about a person's competency in the workplace. "Metabolites?" A metabolite is simply the byproduct *of* the process *of* the degrading *of* a particular chemical compound. So what this means for marijuana is that one doesn't test for THC; one tests for the presence of THC's non-psychoactive *residue*. Here's why the following information is important and why you urgently need to understand this distinction: a urine test that comes back positive for cannabis metabolites will reveal a *history* of pot smoking, but it will not point to a state of being high *right now*. So what's the point in drug testing these people?

Okay, so a commercial pilot doesn't own his aircraft, and so it's understandable why his company, which provides a public service governed by federal regulations, would subject the pilot to certain rules of the air. But deskbound Fortune 500 office workers? Or how about someone who works at Wal-Mart? Well, *used* to work at Wal-Mart.

Joseph Casias, a former Wal-Mart employee, uses marijuana for relief from the pain caused by sinus cancer. Wal-Mart spokesman Greg Rossiter expressed sympathy toward Casias but said, "We have to consider the overall safety of our customers and associates, including Mr. Casias, when making a difficult decision like this." Safety? What reasons did Wal-Mart have to be concerned about safety? Casias had been smoking marijuana for a year to no detriment to anyone else and had maintained a level of responsibility and productivity demanded of him by his employer. Were they afraid he might wander over to the cutlery section and become a knife-wielding maniac?

Wal-Mart refused to rehire Casias. "In states such as Michigan, where prescriptions for marijuana can be obtained, an employer can still enforce a policy that requires termination of employment following a positive drug screen," said one craven dipshit from Wal-Mart's headquarters. Translation: "We don't give a flying fuck if marijuana helps this person suffering from cancer, and we don't give a double flying fuck if he was using marijuana sanctioned by the state of Michigan." Well, you ask, if Casias was not stoned out of his gourd at work, how was his use found out? Good question. He twisted his knee, and company policy has it that all employees who have a workplace injury must undergo a "routine" drug test as a consequence of an on-the-job-related injury. What a world, to get fired for taking medicine.

But here's the real kicker, and we'll see this come into play as marijuana for medical use becomes more prevalent and accepted. If an employed individual who uses marijuana for a medical reason consequently receives dispensation for such use (unlike Joseph Casias) then such dispensation obviously obviates the very reason or need to test for marijuana as a hiring requirement for any prospective employee. You see where I'm going with this: a special dispensation for one smoker—he uses pot for a medical reason (and can still perform the job expected of him)—is a dispensation for all marijuana smokers who use pot recreationally during off hours (and can still perform the job expected of them). Consider an analogy. Right now we could grab a few hundred men in suits off the streets of New York City, throw them into labs as random test subjects, and boringly discover remnants of alcohol from last night's get-together. Shocking news: business people do their fair share of drug taking—drinking—and yet they hold down their jobs. If casual drinking isn't a detriment to climbing ladders, then ditto for pot. Just go ask those stiletto stoners.

"So in your world marijuana is off the hook from drug testing in the nine-to-five workplace. But of course you still want to test for other illegal drugs, right?" Oh boy, here we go. I knew this was coming. Look, we know the war on drugs is mainly about marijuana because pot is the most widely used illicit substance—and therefore the one substance that drug warriors hunt for above all others. But your assertion that I want to "legalize drug abuse" forces me to show my hand. And anyway, there's no way to avoid the question. Every skeptic of marijuana legalization will turn to me and say, "So, do you think cocaine and heroin should be legalized too?" Let me say at the outset of this brief detour—I *really* want to get back to talking about pot—is that if we're going to come to our senses about marijuana it makes little sense to simultaneously deepen our delusions about cocaine and heroin—and, frankly, other illegal drugs.

LET'S START with cocaine (may as well begin alphabetically). Ronald Siegel says "the use of the coca leaf is an Andean tradition dating back thousands of years. The Aymara and Quechua Indians of Bolivia and Peru use coca leaves for cultural, religious, and medicinal purposes. Peasants chew the leaves to combat hunger, thirst, and fatigue, and many natural medicine doctors prescribe coca teas, and coca-based concoctions as remedies for aches, ailments, and digestive problems." Pulverized and mashed into a gooey gob with lime, the coca plant has been enjoyed in this form for generations in South America to no ill effect. Andrew Weil visited Peru and found out for himself when he hung out with some Peruvian pickers. After tucking a gob of this recipe in his cheek he discovered that

> The stuff had a smoky, toasted-green-vegetable flavor. After a few minutes, a pleasant, tingling-numbing sensation pervaded my mouth, and the usual sensations of chewing coca followed: a warm, satisfying feeling in the stomach and a subtle sensation of energy coursing through the body, accompanied by a brightening of mood. ...
>
> I never saw any abuse of coca among these people. They were not addicted to it. Sometimes men of the tribe would hire out as rubber-tree tappers in distant parts of [the Amazon] for six months or a year at a time.

> During those periods, they would be without coca. They missed it, because they liked it, they said, but experienced no difficulty in being away from it. ... The oldest man of the village, in his seventies, was also the heaviest consumer. He could paddle a canoe faster than I could, and was in better physical and mental condition than many seventy-year-olds I see in the United States.

Talk about bringing new meaning to gobsmacked. I have two things to say about this. Number one, I gotta get my hands on this combo, like, *now*. Two, if the Peruvians can manage their coca-chewing habits with care I see no reason why we couldn't do something similar with gum. Really: "energy coursing through the body" accompanied by "a warm, satisfying feeling in the stomach"? C'mon, Wrigley. Do the right thing. Seriously, there's a good reason why coca gum might become a reality one day: coca simply isn't the danger it's chalked up to be. The United States Sentencing Commission noted that "neither powder nor crack cocaine excite[s] or agitate[s] users to commit criminal acts and that the stereotype of a drug-crazed addict committing heinous crimes is not true for either form of cocaine." Slam dunk, that one.

But that's nothing compared to the World Health Organization report from 1995, which… Oops, sorry. The report was suppressed and never published. But here's a taste of the findings, which were issued in a briefing kit. But first, the bona fides and *raison d'etre*: "Between 1992 and 1994 the World Health Organization Programme on Substance Abuse, in association with the United Nations Interregional Crime and Justice Research Institute, undertook the largest global study on cocaine ever." Excellent! And what did they discover?

"Few experts describe cocaine as invariably harmful to health. Cocaine-related problems are widely perceived to be more common and more severe for intensive, high-dosage users and very rare and much less severe for occasional, low-dosage users" and that "occasional cocaine use does not typically lead to severe or even minor physical or social problems. ... Use of coca leaves appears to have no negative health effects and has positive, therapeutic, sacred, and social functions for indigenous Andean populations." Wow. No wonder they killed this report.

They singled out anti-drug ads and campaigns because of the way they "perpetuate stereotypes and misinform the general public." Oh yeah, like those jackasses at The Partnership for a Drug-Free America who equate snorting cocaine with discharging a bullet to the brain via a nasal cavity. If snorting cocaine were akin to shooting a handgun up one's nose, all of Hollywood and half of Wall Street—or is it the other way around?—would be dead by now.

And then the WHO folks hit hard: "Such programs rely on sensationalized, exaggerated statements about cocaine which misinform about patterns of use, stigmatize users, and destroy the educator's credibility." Damn. And you thought coca was an intrinsically debilitating substance for anyone who used it. Sorry, no such luck. "An enormous variety was found in the types of people who use cocaine, the amount of drug used, the frequency of use, the duration and intensity of use, the reasons for using, and any associated problems." It gets worse—for you. "Occasional cocaine use does not typically lead to severe or even minor physical or social problems" and that "experimental and occasional use are by far the most common types of use, and compulsive/dysfunctional is far less common." Better start dismantling your war on cocaine because "approaches which overemphasize punitive drug control measures may actually contribute to the development of health-related problems."

Getting back to you, here you are, looking down the wrong end of the telescope. "Cocaine psychotics are also very acutely paranoid, obsessed with the idea that they are being watched and plotted against." Of *course* these people feel acutely paranoid, you silly goose. They're using an *illegal* drug. They don't want to get caught! Norman Zinberg sees this as self-evident: "In order to deal with the conflict [of not being sure where to get his drug], the user will probably come forth with more bravado, exhibitionism, paranoia, or anti-social feeling than would be the case if he or she had patronized one of the little bars set up alongside the concert hall for the selling of alcohol during intermission." Which isn't to say Carnegie Hall will be offering blow for sale any time soon (and anyway, an energetic pick-me-up might clash with the funereal qualities of Shostakovich's fifteenth string quartet). But you see Zinberg's broader point: if adults were allowed a peaceful means with which to obtain cocaine, paranoia and anti-social feelings would fall by the wayside.

Turning now to the world's most desired illicit opiate, let me start, if I may, with a simple request: enough with the horrors of heroin already. Sure, heroin has its dangers, as does alcohol, in case you forgot, but consuming impure heroin, by definition, is even more dangerous (because, duh, it's *impure*). "Oh, so you're recommending heroin if it were legal?" There you go again, twisting my words around. I didn't say anything about recommending.[*] I'm just pointing to an ineradicable reality: some people in this world are *always* going to play with opiates and so it makes sense that we cater to their desires in a safe manner instead of locking these people up in cages.[**]

Consider this guy who's been snorting heroin two or three times a week for four years. "Why? Why does anybody like anything? I like opiates. It can be done pretty much undetected, without losing your mental abilities." OMG, a rational heroin user! Who let him in the house? Even the reporter who interviewed this guy was taken aback by his levelheadedness, commenting that "nothing in Jeff's manner or conversation betray[ed] the chemical acrobatics taking place within." Exactly. Here, have another: a caller on a television talk show tells us that he visits New York City four or five times a year and

---

[*] Though I will say this. If we lived in a compassionate world the terminally ill would have access to whatever drug they wanted. I don't care if it's heroin. Just give it to them already. This is a human rights issue. Really, the mistreatment of pain is a scandal in this country. Better to die under stuporous conditions than to go out of this world in agony.

[**] You say we "need to have serious consequences or repercussions in place if people use heroin." Why? If a heroin user isn't harming another person, why must there be a repercussion? "States Rethink Drug Laws," N. Koppel and G. Fields, *The Wall Street Journal*, March 5, 2011.

gets "buzzed all night [on heroin] four, five, six times for my eleven-day visit and come back to Michigan without a drug problem. And I don't search for it when I get back here." Wow, *two* rational heroin users. Are there any others?[*]

See, this is what's sad about you. Your yackety-yak about synaptic receptors and dopamine transmitters has you once again looking down the wrong end of the telescope. Studying the neurochemical activity of a drug-addled brain for clues as to why a person finds it difficult to quit smoking, sniffing, drinking, or injecting is like studying the molecular goings-on in the brain of a grieving person who's just lost a loved one to figure out why he's upset. Compulsive, gotta-have-it-now users of whatever recreational drug don't have drug problems; they have *living* problems. To be sure, certain drugs *are* intensely habit-forming, and here's why, in the plainest language I can muster. I apologize for the formality of the following, but I have

---

[*]Yes, there are. A longitudinal study on one hundred and twenty six heroin users conducted in Glasgow revealed that heroin "could indeed be used in a controlled, nonintrusive fashion for an extended period of time" and that "the pharmacological properties of specific substances should not be assumed to inevitably lead to addictive and destructive patterns of drug use."
http://www.doctordeluca.com/Library/AbstinenceHR/ControlledHeroinUseEvidence05.htm

to get professorial on your ass for a moment before I can slay an old dragon of yours.

The human body seeks equilibrium. When a narcotic—such as heroin—is first introduced into the body, it interrupts the routine of a heroin-free, day-to-day level of homeostasis and brings on constipation. With regular and repeated use the body eventually tolerates the drug and constipation ceases to occur, which is another way of saying that the body has transformed itself into a different state of homeostatic equilibrium, one that is now mediated by heroin. Withdrawal, which can be psychologically troubling for some while lethal to others—and, by the way, this applies to alcohol users as well—is simply a case of the body resenting, if you will, the return to the earlier drug-free state. "But doesn't a hardcore heroin user *need* his drug?" Nah, because where recreational drugs are concerned, chemical dependency is a fiction. Hear me out.

SEVERAL YEARS ago an otherwise excellent policy paper on harm reduction noted that many people "view the 'dependence' of former heroin addicts on methadone as practically and ethically indistinguishable from the diabetic's 'dependence' on insulin" (I'll take that opening "many" as a hedge). And for good measure, here's a letter to *The New York Times*: "Why is it a problem if addicts must stay on methadone for the rest of their lives? People with diabetes and epilepsy must take insulin and Dilantin, respectively, all their lives to function properly. In this sense, they are addicted."

I'm all for harm reduction—who could be against distributing clean needles for heroin users? Well, *you* for one though I'm sure you don't object to clean glasses for drinkers. But take a closer look at that policy paper excerpt. Notice how the word dependence twice receives scare quotes as a way to equivalate methadone with insulin. This is inaccurate. Methadone, a synthetic opioid, is just an analog of heroin, the ingestion of which is not necessary for long-term survival (outside of any opiate's efficaciousness as a superb pain killer).

Meanwhile, certain diabetics *will* die without a constant supply of insulin, and epileptics can avoid seizures only by taking anticonvulsants such as phenytoin sodium or lamotrogine. But there is simply no corollary for heroin users. As much as you would like to believe otherwise, there's never any moment in any heroin user's life where he reaches some point of no return, where he now has to take heroin for the rest of his life.

Millions of people have taken opiates to relieve pain from an injury or operation—and then stopped using when they recovered. Many servicemen in the Vietnam War took heroin to stave off stress—but gave up the drug when they returned home. No, I'm not belittling the seriously troubled user, whose withdrawal might need medical supervision. All I'm saying is that the notion of heroin-dependent—or alcohol-dependent—people is bogus, but that insulin-dependent people truly exist in the world. Moving on.

You insist that long-term drug users lack free will because they are "hooked" on whatever drug that "hijacks" the brain. Nonsense. Instead of destroying free will, habitual drug use *reinforces* free will. Think about it. Every time a smoker or drinker reaches for a cigarette or a glass of booze he knows exactly what he's doing—and indeed has to in order to get his desired hit of nicotine or alcohol. And, predictably enough, when a person quits smoking or drinking, a Proustian longing for the drug in question often comes on.

Several years ago *60 Minutes* interviewed a former tobacco executive stricken with smoking-related cancer who said he still craved a cigarette even years after not smoking—that is, long after nicotine had been flushed from his body. As he put it, "I can still remember how great it was in the morning with that cup of coffee and a cigarette. If it wasn't for this, the cancer, I'd be smoking." But fondly recalling an old habit is not a disease. Or in the words of L. Rust Hills, "longing for a cigarette is one of the least aimless longings there is." And if gratification can be derived from such an aimless longing, who's surprised that a smoker feels doubly empty when he's *not* smoking?

But there's a deeper problem here, and it's one that goes beyond any discussion of "reward centers" in the brain. The blurring of unrelated categories—protein corruptions and cellular pathologies with problems in living and existential turmoil—helps to explain why Mary Tyler Moore once said she inherited her mother's alcoholism. Certainly Ms. Moore's claim can't be the same as Julie Andrews saying that arthritis runs in her family. People with arthritis are unwilling victims of an inflammatory disorder. People with life-destroying drinking habits are willing participants in their self-destruction—and besides, if a person learns he *has* inherited a particular sensitivity to alcohol, then such knowledge *ups* the ante of responsibility.

Think it through. If you're told you have a predisposition to booze in that liquor can make you tipsy more quickly than other people who are not so predisposed, well, armed with such knowledge, you are now *more* responsible for not drinking or for not drinking excessively—which is to also say that a sodden lout who punches a woman in the face does so not because of how his body processes alcohol but because he's a jerk. Yes, drinking can be a handmaiden to violence, but it's also true that many long-term heavy drinkers will simply sink into a private morass of despair and self-loathing.

John Cheever in his journals tells us how easily he could be set off at a moment's slight toward his liquor cabinet: "I find these rebuffs a serious depressant and, using this as an excuse, I take a little gin with my orange juice." This was not a man with a brain disease but a sensitive individual with a profound problem in living. Or to put this in a fictional light, Martin Amis noted the following of his protagonist in *The Information*: "These days he smoked and drank largely to solace himself for what drinking and smoking had done to him—but smoking and drinking had done a lot to him, so he drank and smoked a lot." Perfect.

Here's another way to look at this. Think of natural selection as having "built" the experience of depression into us as a warning signal that something is not right with our existential situation.* Hunger is a sign that one needs to eat, fatigue of the ordinary end-of-day kind is a sign that one needs to rest, and depression is a sign that one's existential relationship to the world has gone off the rails and urgently needs to be righted—and when a person is unwilling to face up to a problem in living, a psychoactive drug is often used as an escape from the mind-crushing issue at hand.** But we know as a fact of life that no one *needs* alcohol or heroin or any recreational drug to survive, whereas just try going without food and water. So the idea of "chemical dependency" runs counter to a paradox of life: it's unhappiness, a lack of satisfaction in life, that drives us on to live—and when that unhappiness is particularly deep and long-lasting some people will turn to drugs as a way to assuage their existential plight. So you can't come at me and say that a moderate drinker

---

*The problem with chemical imbalances as an explanation for the cause of depression is a problem of differential diagnosis. We can determine whether a person has hay fever or a cold, but we have no way of ascertaining that a chemical imbalance causes depression. Or to put this as a question, when a chemical imbalance is broached as a cause for depression, how exactly is it determined that a person is *not* suffering from a profound problem in living?

**If a drug such as Prozac can "jump-start someone out of a depression," as Jonathan Lear has asked, "does the person use the relief from crippling pain as an opportunity to work through the meanings and conflicts inherent in his life; or is he 'relieved' of that opportunity?" It's a good question. J. Lear, *Love and Its Place in Nature* (New York: Farrar, Straus & Giroux, 1990), p. 21.

is exercising responsible, willful behavior but that a person who plows through a bottle of whatever on a nightly basis is in the grip of a chemical slavery. Look at your contradiction. On one hand you say heavy drinkers have a disease that robs them of their free will; and on the other, you say that abstinence—*choosing* not to drink (exercising free will)—is the only solution to their problem.

Here's the skinny. Drug habits don't develop into diseases; they develop into bad habits.* Theories of compulsive drug users in the grip of a disease are not advancements in medicine but a degradation of our ideas of freedom—and a freedom that includes, by definition, the possibility of going down a tortured path whose end point is self-destruction. Sorry, that's life. Well, it's certainly one aspect of the *tragic* side of life. And when we admit to this reality of mind and choice—that to take that last drink means one has *chosen* to stop drinking—we are left with a question that collapses on its own absurdity: by what definition of medicine is *not* taking a drug a cure for a disease?

YOU'LL BE PLEASED to know that some progress has been made on creating a vaccine to

---

*Though excessive drinking, for example, can certainly lead to some bona fide diseases, such as cirrhosis of the liver or cancer.

block the effects of cocaine (and apparently there's also one underway for nicotine users). Let me see if I understand this correctly. Joe the Addict has an intense craving for cocaine. But Joe, being a good guy at heart, wants to beat this craving. He is now presented with two choices. Either Joe, or his medical insurance company, or even more likely the state, will pay exorbitant sums of dollars for generous servings of this new miraculous substance, which, presumably, will be called AntiCo (it would be labeled AntiCoke were it not for copyright infringement). Joe receives an injection of AntiCo. Then, after inhaling or smoking cocaine, he doesn't satisfy his craving because AntiCo will have neutralized cocaine's effects. When the effects of both AntiCo and cocaine have worn off, Joe will repeat the process. And repeat it again and again. Until he gets it right—until, that is, he's overcome his craving for cocaine. In effect, he's gone cold turkey.

Choice number two: he goes cold turkey. He obtains (that is, pays for or has somebody else pay for) no AntiCo. He obtains (that is, pays for or has somebody else pay for) no cocaine. He suffers the pangs of going without cocaine. Total cost to the taxpayer? Nada, zilch, zero. But Joe, driven on by the recommendations of his political leaders, his doctors, the drug companies, and the drug-treatment experts, chooses, of course, option one. Should this "cure" pan out, we can look forward to an escalation of the drug war as the most incorrigible of users seek out more cocaine in an attempt to outdo the strength of the catalyst. Delightful.

And for those who won't go cold turkey, there is another kind of "treatment" available. But first, I would like to pause here and provide an example of the proper use of the word "treatment." From the "Science Times" section of *The New York Times*: "Like pneumonia, dental decay results from a bacterial infection that does not go away without treatment." Perfect. Treatment, by definition, cannot be verbal; it is either pharmacological in application, such as antibiotics for pneumonia, or it is directly physical, such as inserting a stent into a coronary artery—or removing bacterial plaque from teeth.

But for certain chronic users of rock cocaine, treatment takes on a unique form. Check it out: "In a single therapy session, patients sit and dip out one cupful of water and examine its contents. One cup represents a measure of the tears we cry in a single therapy session as we gradually heal ourselves by both describing traumatic memories and feeling the original affective we felt at the time of our traumas. This process may take some people two years and others may need four, five, or more years of therapy gradually to heal themselves, depending on the number of buckets they carry." I marvel at the precision of this cure. But I have to say I'm curious to know just how many buckets of lachrymal excretions objectively represent the amount of tears "needed" to cry.

Let's give the last word on this topic to *The New York Times* by way of a headline of theirs that's worthy of *The Onion*: "Anti-Smoking Spray Helps But is Addictive." The comedy never ends.

RETURNING TO YOUR *bête noire*, you said I'm nuts to think any good could come from inhaling burning plant matter. I understand how you could arrive at this assumption. Tobacco is smoked; marijuana is smoked. Tobacco causes cancer; ergo, marijuana must also cause cancer. If the latter were true, Jamaica would be a veritable cancer ward by now. But an editorial from *The Lancet*, a leading medical journal, declared that "the smoking of cannabis, even long term, is not harmful to health." Let's take a closer look.

The National Institute on Drug Abuse funded Donald Tashkin, a medical professor at the University of California, Los Angeles, for a study that NIDA hoped would reveal that marijuana smoking causes lung cancer. Tashkin rudely reported back that marijuana does *not* cause lung cancer and does *not* promote COPD, chronic obstructive pulmonary disease, thus dashing the prohibitionist delusions—excuse me, dreams—of NIDA. As Tashkin noted, the findings "were against our expectations." And that's not all. "We know that there are as many or more carcinogens and co-carcinogens in marijuana smoke as in cigarettes, but we did not find any evidence for an increase in cancer risk for even heavy marijuana smoking." Tashkin has company.

Here's Hal Morgenstern at the University of Michigan School of Public Health. "We had hypothesized, based on prior laboratory evidence, including animal studies, that long-term heavy use of marijuana would increase the risk of lung and head and neck cancers, but we didn't get any evidence of that."

"But marijuana kills brain cells!" Heh. This idea got started with the (in)famous Heath/Tulane University study of 1974. The study showed that marijuana killed brain cells of Rhesus monkeys, but, as was discovered years later, these brain cell deaths were not due to marijuana inhalation per se but to *suffocation*. See, the hapless simians wore gas masks and had mega amounts of marijuana pumped into them. So, the monkeys die from suffocation, the first cells to die when suffocation occurs are brains cells, and voilà, you have a "study" showing that marijuana kills brain cells. Fantastic.

Nicotine? Nicotine patches "appear to *promote* the spread and re-growth of cancer tumors." Yes, you read that right: not the mere inhalation of nicotine but *patches*. On the *skin*. Christopher Forsyth, an assistant professor of medicine and biochemistry at Rush University Medical Center, discovered "that alcohol turns on certain signals inside a cell" via an "epithelial-to-mesenchymal transition," which simply means that localized cancer cells are turned into aggressive tumor cells that can spread quickly throughout the body. Marijuana? Not only does pot *not* kill brain cells, it has been shown in some preliminary studies to *promote* the growth of brain cells. A study at the University of Saskatchewan showed that a synthetic analog to THC stimulated brain growth in rats. And over at Ohio State University a study revealed that "a marijuana-based medicine triggered the formation of new brain cells and cut inflammation linked to dementia."*

---

*Maybe all this helps to explain why Anderson Cooper said, by his own admission, that he got "crushed" by Cheech Marin on *Celebrity Jeopardy*. I'd call that a solid anecdote.

Anju Preet, at Harvard University, presented this startling finding to the American Association for Cancer Research: marijuana stunted the growth of cancerous lung tumors in lab rats. Preet explains that with the body's own cannabinoid system "THC activates two specific endocannabinoids that are present in high amounts of lung cancer cells. This revs up their natural anti-inflammatory properties, an extremely important finding, because inflammation can promote the growth and spread of cancer."

The British Journal of Cancer reports that Dr. Ines Diaz-Laviada and her colleagues at the University of Alcala in Madrid found that certain chemicals in cannabis "can stop the division and growth of prostate cancer cells and could become a target for new research into potential drugs to treat prostate cancer."

Have another, from the journal *Molecular Cancer.* Quoting directly from their highly technical paper, titled "Cannabinoids reduce ErbB2-driven breast cancer progression through Akt inhibition": "The purpose of this study was to determine whether cannabinoids might constitute a new therapeutic tool for the treatment of ErbB2-positive breast tumors. We analyzed their antitumor potential in a well-established and clinically relevant model of ErbB2-driven metastatic breast cancer: the MMTV-neu mouse. We also analyzed the expression of cannabinoid targets in a series of eighty-seven human breast tumors." Hmm. Very interesting. And what did they discover? "Our results show that both Δ^9-tetrahydro-cannabinol, the most abundant and potent cannabinoid in marijuana, and JWH-133, a nonpsychotropic CB_2 receptor-selective agonist, reduce tumor growth, tumor number, and the amount/severity of lung metastases in MMTV-neu mice."

Have another. Researchers at Complutense University in Spain discovered THC causes brain cancer cells to undergo autophagy. And what, pray, does this ugly word mean? "Autophagy is a breakdown of a cell that occurs when the cell essentially self-digests." Translation: marijuana promotes the *death* of brain cancer cells. Yeah, you didn't see that one coming.

"But we know for sure THC use can lead to psychosis." You're getting desperate now. At the Harplands Psychiatric Hospital in the township of Hartshill, England, researchers discovered—with the help of one hundred and eighty-three general practitioners and hundreds of thousands of patients already diagnosed with various kinds of psychoses—that marijuana did *not* increase or amplify psychotic states of mind. Not good enough for you? A similar study from the United Kingdom, one comprising six hundred thousand individuals, investigated the notion that cannabis in the 1970s would lead to an increase in the number of schizophrenics twenty years later. "Between 1996 and 2005 the incidence and prevalence of schizophrenia and psychoses were either stable or declining" and that "in conclusion, this study did not find any evidence of increasing schizophrenia or psychoses in the general population from 1996 to 2005."

On another matter entirely, the American Glaucoma Society admits in a position statement that marijuana can be helpful for those who suffer from interocular pressure (glaucoma), but adds a caveat: "Marijuana's mood-altering effects would prevent the patient who is using it from driving, operating heavy machinery, and functioning at maximum mental capacity." To which Russ Belville of NORML notes, "You know what else prevents people from driving and operating heavy machinery? Blindness."

Thanks to the Mayo Clinic, we have a solid understanding of conventional eyedrop medications of various strengths and types. Here's a list of their side effects alongside those of cannabis:

Eye-Drop Medications	Cannabis
• Lower blood pressure	• Slightly lower blood pressure, leading to…
• Dizziness	• Slightly increased heart rate
• Impotence	• Mood-altering effects
• Frequent urination	• Dry mouth
• Weakness	• Hunger
• Red, itchy or swollen eyes	• Bloodshot eyes
• Pain around or inside eyes	
• Blurred or dim vision	
• Difficulty breathing	
• Fatigue	
• Brow ache	
• Hair loss	
• Sweating	
• Headache	

Oh, and assuming you're *smoking* pot, let's not forget the dreaded halitosis.

So tell me, if you had glaucoma, would you rather have mood-altering effects and dry mouth or would you go with the impotence and hair loss? Just asking.

But take another look at that table. These effects aren't happening on some mythical "side"; they're *direct* effects. Look, if you take a prescription drug for some ailment and discover that it also causes gas, headache, or heartburn or you take a different drug to relieve something else and come down with a rash, hives, or itching, these undesired reactions—some scary, others *very* scary, and some fatal—are the *total* effects of the drug.

Consider two popular drugs that are used by the over-sixty crowd (mostly) for a different recreational purpose. I'm speaking, of course, of Viagra and Cialis. Take a look at the "side" effects that are said to be "rare": "sudden decrease or loss of hearing" and "sudden decrease or loss of vision." Not to worry, because "the most common side effects of Viagra are headache, facial flushing, and upset stomach. Less commonly, bluish vision, blurred vision, or sensitivity to light may briefly occur." In other words, only have sex in the dark and then throw up.

From the Cialis Web site: "Stop sexual activity and get medical help right away if you get symptoms such as chest pain, dizziness, or nausea during sex." Huh. "Stop sexual activity." It seems to me sexual activity stops when our bodies reach a certain age and tell us that fun time is over. But erectile drugs keep up, as it were, the illusion that a guy can naturally fuck his way into his nineties. My heart goes out to all the young arm candy who want to land elder sugar daddies. But I digress.

Hey, have trouble sleeping? You can always take Lunesta. "Severe allergic reactions such as swelling of the tongue and throat occur rarely and may be fatal"—or, if you want a good night's sleep without choking to death, you could take a couple of hits of weed.

Fibromyalgia? Pfizer tells us "Lyrica may cause swelling of your hands, legs, and feet, which can be serious for people with heart problems. Lyrica may cause dizziness and sleepiness. Also, tell your doctor right away about muscle pain or problems along with feeling sick and feverish, or any changes in your eyesight including blurry vision or if you have any kidney problems or get dialysis." Marijuana? Call the following message-board comments anecdotal; I call them genuine comments from people who a) are in real pain and b) are not bullshitting us.

> Marijuana helps me with multiple symptoms. I have fibromyalgia, irritable bowel syndrome, arthritis, depression, etc. I'm on a lot of prescribed medications, but marijuana helps the muscle pain of fibromyalgia much more than the Ultram and Flexeryl I am prescribed. Even Vicodin does not relieve the kind of pain I experience.

I've had fibromyalgia for four years. I have been on every kind of painkiller imaginable, and I must mention that I have ended up in the hospital for taking them. Fibromyalgia is real! I have tried marijuana for the first time after doing much research. I personally have found it impossible to smoke. I have never smoked anything in my life, and the first puff I took was terrible. I coughed so hard that I vomited. But what did however work was eating it. I found that all the spasms stopped. I was relaxed for the first time in four years, and I got a solid eleven hours of well-deserved sleep. In my opinion, marijuana is a safe, effective drug, and when taken responsibly, can change your life, or in my case, give me my life back.

I've found it to be extremely beneficial in relaxing very tightened muscles and severe fibro pain. Nothing else the doctor has prescribed has worked as well as marijuana (although I do not have a prescription). I had a major meltdown last night. Was in severe pain, having anxiety issues due to pain and was just crying and at the end of my rope once again because the fibro has ruined my formerly active life. My husband filled a pipe for me and in just two tokes, I was calm, relaxed, my muscle tension eased, and I was asleep in about twenty minutes. I had a restful night's sleep for the first time in days. I had been struggling with marijuana use, but now, I know that it is definitely helping; I think the struggle is over and I will turn to this more.

Yes, some folks with fibromyalgia have said they haven't had much success with pot. But I have a hunch. The problem may not be with the supposed ineffectiveness of marijuana but with marijuana's *illegal* status, because prohibition leaves users in the dark about what they're getting. But in places where marijuana has been legalized for medical use, caregivers and consultants can educate users on the varying strains, strengths, and uses of cannabis.

Cannabis comes in two major strains (Ruderalis isn't significant because it has little THC): Indica, which is preferable for relieving pain (due to its reputation for bringing on a state of bodily relaxation); and Sativa, which brings on a more cerebral, excited-mind high. When writers or musicians speak of a high that gets them motivated and thinking, it's because they probably smoked Sativa; individuals who say they feel sleepy or relaxed have probably smoked Indica. As for individuals with medical conditions who say they haven't experienced relief from using pot, it's probably because they have smoked the wrong (or a weak) strain.

And whose fault is it that these people are smoking the wrong strain? That's easy to answer: you. *Maybe* marijuana isn't ideal for *all* people with fibromyalgia, but we'll never really know for sure as long as people have to resort to an underground "market" where unlabeled strains—is it Indica? is it Sativa?—are unhelpfully out there. Nevertheless, take a look at some glowing testimonies.

Joni Whiting testified at Minnesota's Public Safety Policy and Oversight Committee as part of the state's decision to consider a provision to provide marijuana for medicinal use. She told the story of her daughter's facial melanoma and how Stephanie's nausea and agonizing pain were *not* relieved by any prescription drug but only by smoked marijuana. At first Stephanie was wary of procuring a banned substance, but after the urging of Stephanie's siblings, "I [the mother] called a number of family members and friends and asked if they knew of anywhere we could purchase marijuana. The next morning someone had placed a package of it on our doorstep. I have never known whom to thank for it but I remain grateful beyond belief." She concluded her presentation to the legislative committee by saying she would have had "no problem going to jail for acquiring medical marijuana for my suffering child."

Paul Bowles once said that he liked smoking marijuana because it helped to "let the subconscious take over," which is just another way of saying that pot brings on an illuminative, free-floating state of mind. If marijuana can amplify a writer's default state of free association, I can see how marijuana might lessen an autistic person's self-absorption. Guess what? There's at least one mother who is giving marijuana to her autistic child (in brownies), and she finds that pot is transforming her son for the better.

Marie Myung-Ok Lee's nine-year-old son has autism, and as a way to lessen his tantrums at school, she decided not to give her son Risperdal, the most popular "anti-psychotic" medication for children after she learned that its long-term viability still hadn't been verified *and* because she learned that forty-five pediatric deaths were attributed to the drug. She also put the kibosh on the drug after discovering on her own that parents of other children who had autism told her that they saw no improvement with Risperdal.

After some trepidation she and her husband finally went with marijuana (nice to know that the state she lives in, Rhode Island, supports the use of marijuana for medical reasons). Initially her son seemed to like marijuana-laden cookies but then rejected them. Ms. Lee then turned to making a marijuana tea with goji berries—and with that she hit on a formula that worked like magic for her son: fewer aggression-fueled episodes, better nights sleeping, and a warmer relationship with Grandma, who agreed that the concoction improved the boy's attention span and communication skills tremendously. The real evidence of marijuana's success? The absence of pica, an eating disorder whereby people will eat and nibble at non-nutritive substances. Ms. Lee said that her son always used to come home with his shirt in shreds, but after she got him started on marijuana, the pica stopped.

Even more exciting, her son was subjected to a therapy called Applied Behavioral Analysis, which kept track of aggressive episodes at school (hitting, biting, and so on). Prior to using marijuana her son had "thirty to fifty aggressions in a school day." And what was the number a few months later after the routine of ingesting marijuana settled in? *Zero*. There's more: "In four months, he'd gone from a boy we couldn't feed to a boy who could feed himself and clean up after." As for other prescription medications, "the drugs that our insurance would pay for—and that the people around us would support without question—pose real risks to children. For now, we're sticking with the weed."

Wow, news reports like these, while I know they can't touch your lizard heart, really must stick in your craw because they conflict with your medical paradigm, which argues that marijuana can't ever be a medicine because real medicine entails creating or synthesizing chemicals in a laboratory and then distributing these discoveries and inventions in precise dosages as capsules, pills, liquids, or powders.

I see your point, particularly with regard to measurable dosages. There's no question that it's helpful to know that an aspirin tablet or an ibuprofen capsule in my hand contains two hundred milligrams of the drug and not two thousand. This is all fine and good—and necessary for laboratory-made drugs.

But there's no arguing with reality: smoked cannabis just happens to be the ideal "drug delivery device," to use your argot, of tetrahydrocannabinol. I know this must infuriate you but you're just gonna have to suck it up. Raw marijuana is indeed a genuine outlier that goes against the grain of modern medicine.* "I Can't Believe It's Not Marijuana" just isn't the tag line for prescription

---

*And if the imprecision of dosage seems like bad medicine (or not medicine at all) to you, how do you explain the medical use of maggots for gangrene ulcers? How about leeches? They're used to drain blood after reconstructive surgery. Doctors can even buy "medical-grade leeches" from a firm called Leeches U.S.A. Ltd.

Marinol. Nobody's buying it, literally and figuratively (except for those who don't like to smoke or who want to smoke but are afraid of getting in trouble with the law). These people don't want synthetic THC; they want the real deal. They tell us again and again that Marinol is slow-acting and weak and that smoked marijuana, because it's inhaled, gets to the problem quickly and more effectively. Besides, do you really think you can argue your case with Jacqueline Patterson?

Check out *In Pot We Trust*, a Showtime documentary from some years back. Patterson has cerebral palsy, and in the film we see her struggling to speak, with frequent and long "ummmmm"s punctuating her speech. So with pipe in hand, she ignites the bowl, takes a few hits—and a seeming magical transformation occurs in mere seconds. Where prior to smoking we saw her speak only in fits and starts we now see a fluency in conversation unimaginable before she lit up. It's as if the volume control for her symptoms was turned down several notches (some people with Parkinson's report experiencing the same thing). Patterson says that by the third hit or so she feels an immediate dissipation of tension. No, marijuana is not a cure for this woman, but it does provide a measure of relief. Who would deny her that?

Her government, that's who. Here's what's galling. The Drug Enforcement Administration maintains that marijuana has no medical value all the while ignoring (or cynically in cahoots with) another arm of government that claims otherwise. No, make that *two* arms. I told you it was galling.

THE COMPASSIONATE Investigational New Drug Study began in 1978 (and no *investigations* as such were ever conducted) as a response to a lawsuit filed by Robert Randall, who was going blind. He filed a brief arguing by way of the Common Law doctrine of medical necessity that marijuana was necessary for *him*. On November 24, 1976, federal Judge James Washington came down with his ruling and said the following: "While blindness was shown by competent medical testimony to be the otherwise inevitable result of the defendant's disease, no adverse effects from the smoking of marijuana have been demonstrated. Medical evidence suggests that the medical prohibition is not well founded."

Which takes us to Irvin Rosenfeld, who suffers from a rare bone disorder, multiple congenital cartilaginous exostoses, and is one of the few remaining members of a program that was inexplicably shut down for new entrants in 1982. Since that year the federal government has been sending Mr. Rosenfeld a monthly tin of rolled marijuana cigarettes. That's pretty cool. What's not cool is that the government has seen to it that the buds of the plant (where the most concentrated amounts of THC are to be found) are removed, thereby leading to rolled joints that are made primarily of leaves and stems, which have weak(er) traces of THC. It's hard to say if this is the government acting out a cruel revenge for getting slapped in the face by a federal judge or because Inspector Clouseau is in charge of the fed's marijuana-distribution system. But here's what you need to know: Rosenfeld smokes about a dozen joints per day, he works as a stockbroker, his co-workers speak well of him, and—pardon me as I throw a wrench into your gears of prohibitionist thinking—*he drives to and from work every day.* (I'll have more to say about high driving in a bit.)

In a press release sent out on November 20, 2009, to announce his record of smoking his 115,000th joint—which, by the way, was also the twenty-seventh anniversary of his first shipment of a tin of pre-rolled joints from Uncle Sam (he receives three hundred and sixty joints per month)—Rosenfeld said the following: "I cannot fathom the reluctance of my federal government to allow the use of medical cannabis for the sick and dying. My experience of use, the calming of my negative symptoms, that has allowed me to be a useful, contributing member of society must be extended to all the ill based on the judgment of medical professionals and not guided or restrained by the dictates of law enforcement who have no empathy for the ill nor the education to appropriately enter into doctor-patient relationships and treatment options."

Now, since I wrote you last, some exciting things have occurred. The American Medical Association now supports the medical use of marijuana. For seventy-plus years this venerable (and conservative) institution maintained that marijuana had no medical or therapeutic value. But in November of 2009, the organization issued a press release, in advance of a forthcoming and more detailed explanation, indicating that *smoked* marijuana *does* have some medical benefits, and as a result of this decision, the organization is now recommending that the Drug Enforcement Administration, with its reliance on the Controlled Substances Act, reschedule the drug as a plant from having no medicinal value, Schedule I, to Schedule II, where medicinal benefits can be studied by researchers without fear of the DEA's stormtroopers barging in and making arrests.

Now, the Controlled Substances Act, passed into law in 1970, is perhaps the most significant piece of legislation by prohibitionists in modern times. Do you remember how this law came to be? Timothy Leary—yes, *that* Timothy Leary—was arrested for marijuana possession, a violation of the Marihuana Tax Act. Leary challenged the Act on the grounds that it required self-incrimination and therefore was in violation of the Fifth Amendment. The court agreed and declared by unanimous decision that Leary's "conviction under the Marihuana Tax Act violated his privilege against self-incrimination." Whoa, hold on there a sec, fellas. Violated his *privilege* against self-incrimination? It's not a privilege, you saps. It's a *right*. But the government still alleged that marijuana was dangerous stuff, and so after tossing out the Marihuana Tax Act they created the Controlled Substances Act. Drunken idiot elves must have written this thing. Just take a look at this legal mishmash.

The Act segregates drugs into five incoherent and contradictory categories. Marijuana is a Schedule I drug (the most dangerous), but cocaine is not (due to limited medical use) and is in Schedule II. Get this:

cocaine can kill you; marijuana cannot. Over-the-counter aspirin? It's not even scheduled. It's off the chart, as it were—and yet aspirin kills five thousand people a year, whereas marijuana... must I repeat myself? And now for some really discouraging news.

More than twenty years ago DEA Chief Administrative Law Judge Francis L. Young argued that marijuana should be moved from Schedule I to Schedule II. "Marijuana, in its natural form," said the judge in his Marijuana Rescheduling Petition on September 6, 1988, "is one of the safest therapeutically active substances known to man. By any measure of rational analysis marijuana can be safely used within a supervised routine of medical care." Young's findings were met with silence—and the scheduling system continued on its loony way. Take a look: Marinol is synthetic THC (remember, *marijuana*'s THC is said to have no medical benefits) and a Schedule III drug; CBD, a cannabinoid, is a *non*psychoactive drug, but a Schedule I drug. GHB, once freely available, is now said to have no medical use and is therefore a Schedule I drug—oh, but hold on: an exception is made for narcolepsy. Yes, this is your government hard at work.

Although you love to maintain that there's no such thing as medical use for pot[*] despite the avalanche of facts that prove you wrong, there's no question that "medical marijuana" is finally having its day. Fantastic—and yet I wince at that phrase "medical marijuana" for two reasons. First, I fear that it might eventually be used as a bludgeon against recreational pot smokers: average people everywhere, along with many famous creative people we revere—actors, musicians, writers, and so on—would be accused of breaking medical marijuana "prescription" laws. Second, it's ludicrous to think that in this late stage of our civilization sweepstakes that we are in special need of trained physicians to dole out a plant that grows like *and is* a weed. Now don't get me wrong. There's nothing wrong with soliciting help. I think it was Gore Vidal who once said that the two things in life we know the least about are taxes and our bodies, and so it makes some practical sense to have a professional intermediary give us guidance on medical matters. But note that in those states where cannabis is legal for medical use doctors do not *prescribe* marijuana. Why?

---

[*] I just love quoting you: "This is not medicine, this is a Cheech and Chong show." *CNN Presents: Higher Times*, January 5, 1997. That Cheech and Chong only made *movies* and not TV shows (and had never toured until 2008) proves just how out of touch you are.

Because marijuana is a plant, not a synthesized, laboratory-made chemical governed by FDA regulations. Consequently, doctors *recommend* marijuana. This is fine insofar that it is a step up from the infantilization imposed on us by an authoritarian medical bureaucracy.* But consider just how backward we are: for a plant that has been used widely and agreeably for all sorts of medicinal reasons for the first twenty centuries of the Common Era (at least), it's now considered "progressive" in the twenty-first for an intermediary in a white coat to hand us a faux "prescription" for it. This is a joke.

See, the appeal of marijuana centers on two facts of life, though it tends to be the case that the first is rarely mentioned publicly (unless you happen to be Lady Gaga): getting high can be creatively and intellectually stimulative; and two, the plant is helpful for alleviating a wide variety of medical conditions, as we saw with Jacqueline Patterson and other individuals. Heaven forfend that the two should ever meet, that a person

*My blast here at our prescription laws is rooted in the following. I understand the need for safety and caution, and while it may be necessary to talk to a doctor in order to get his expertise on needed medications to resolve a problem, I don't want his *permission* to use a drug; I want his *advice*. To put this plainly, as a competent adult who is not a ward of the state, I can *read labels* and *follow directions*.

suffering from cancer and wanting to ward off nausea might not mind the high.*

But when the photographer Robert Frank tells *The New York Times* "I smoke it to relax," who are we to say that his smoking is "merely" recreational? You relax with a glass of wine; Frank relaxes with a joint. Many of us also bifurcate the use of food: you can "recreationally" consume certain items because they're delicious and enjoyable, and you can also consume them because they're good for health. Question: do we speak of "medical food" or do we just speak of food?

Blueberries are delicious in my morning oatmeal—and they also have antioxidant and anti-inflammatory properties. They're also good for vision health. Medical blueberries, anyone? It's been suggested that resveratol, found in red wine, is good for the heart. Medical red wine, anyone? Millions of people drink coffee every morning to bring on an extra state of alertness (hmm, sounds vaguely medical to me), while others use it to ward off asthma. Hell, some people have coffee

---

*And then there's Stephen Jay Gould, who underwent chemotherapy during one of his last bouts with cancer, and because of the nausea that resulted from the treatment he decided to smoke some pot. Gould said it worked like a charm, but he disliked the "mental blurring" (as he called it)—which he also noted was the main effect for recreational users. So the high, from Gould's perspective, was the undesirable "side effect"! That's funny. L. Grinspoon and J. Bakakar, *Marihuana: The Forbidden Medicine* (New Haven: Yale University Press, 1993), p. 38.

enemas. Medical coffee, anyone? Enough already with "medical" marijuana. It doesn't exist. There's only *marijuana* and nothing else. See, the issue isn't that pot is safer than alcohol (though it is); nor is it that THC is useful for people with certain medical conditions (though it is). The issue is that marijuana has *multiple* uses, which renders moot the notion that it's only good or useful for one (medical) purpose. If you smoke pot for mental stimulation, fine. If you smoke it to fall asleep, fine. And as for Jacqueline Patterson, she's perfectly capable of deciding on her own what she wants to do with the plant. She doesn't need *permission* from a doctor to use a common weed. She needs to be *left alone* to do what she will to make her life pleasant and as enjoyable as possible.

A few paragraphs back I said there are two arms of government that make a claim for the medical efficaciousness of marijuana. The first was the Compassionate Investigational New Drug Study. Here's the second arm, the crème de la crème of nefarious or nitwitted (take your pick) government.

Here you go: patent number 6,630,507, issued on October 7, 2003, by the Patent and Trademark Office: "Cannabinoids as antioxidants and neuroprotectants." The patent notes that cannabinoids are medically useful for individuals suffering from stroke, trauma, autoimmune disorders, Alzheimer's, HIV dementia, and Parkinson's. Here's the kicker. The patent was awarded to—you are not going to believe this; get ready to pick your jaw up from the floor—"The United States of America as represented by the Department of Health and Human Services" (quoting directly from the patent). Yes, you read that right: the United States *government* essentially issued this patent to *itself*.

One skeptical commentator, who goes by the cheery name of James Bong, wrote this apt comment in response to the issuance: "You can't patent cannabis any more than you can patent the multiplication tables or mockingbirds. Patents have to be unique inventions, not attempts to monopolize nature or logic. There are limits to the patentability of objects, and nearly all of them have been exceeded here, for a multiplicity of reasons." In the meantime, we have a sequel in 7,109,245: "Vasoconstrictor cannabinoid analogs."

So let's review. THC, the active ingredient in marijuana, has no medical value and yet Marinol exists; smoked marijuana has no medical value and yet Mr. Rosenfeld receives "medical marijuana" (though it appears to be schwag) from the federal government; a Drug

Enforcement Administration judge says in 1988 that "marijuana, in its natural form, is one of the safest therapeutically active substances known to man" and yet the agency continues to maintain that marijuana has no medical value—and all of this happening as the government quietly pursues cannabinoid-related patents in the hope that it can one day cash in on the windfall from the tax-rich world of legal marijuana. Coming from the government, this is all pretty amazing, especially for its chutzpah. But all these confusions and disconnects, to put it mildly, can only mean one thing: marijuana prohibition is on its last legs.

NEAR THE END of our War on Liquor, the wealthy industrialist, John D. Rockefeller, Jr., one of Prohibition's early supporters, confessed to the failure of banning alcohol. Here he is, in a letter from 1932:

> "When Prohibition was introduced, I hoped that it would be widely supported by public opinion and the day would soon come when the evil effects of alcohol would be recognized. I have slowly and reluctantly come to believe that this has not been the result. Instead, drinking has generally increased; the speakeasy has replaced the saloon; a vast army of lawbreakers has appeared; many of our best citizens have openly ignored Prohibition; respect for the

> law has been greatly lessened; and crime has increased to a level never seen before."

It's nice that Rockefeller could admit to the error of his ways. But notice his unstated assumption. He still thinks prohibiting alcohol is, in theory, a good idea, but admits that the war on alcohol didn't work. Sound familiar? You often hear lazy-minded legalizers say the war on drugs "is not working." This is a peculiar thing to say because it suggests that in the best of all possible worlds the war on drugs could work or ought to work. But women didn't acquire the right to vote because the laws preventing them from doing so "no longer worked." Slavery didn't end because the laws for that foul institution "no longer worked." Blanch at that last comparison, but I'm holding my ground: the war on drugs is easily and without a doubt *the* worst social policy in the United States—and in the world, with my country 'tis of thee leading this ignoble cause—since the end of slavery. It isn't that the drug war isn't working. It's that the drug war is *wrong*.

Oh, but there you go, arguing that legalization is nothing more than a case of saying "if you cannot conquer an evil, become part of it." You speak of ending the war on marijuana as a "surrender" and how legalization should be regarded as a "dangerous experiment." Nope. Give yourself a booby prize. *Prohibition* is the dangerous experiment. Ending the war against marijuana means returning to a pre-prohibition norm that existed for thousands of years. Ending prohibition is not about appeasing or surrendering to drug gangs; it's about putting the drug gangs out of business.

What's more, in your screwy up-is-down/down-is-up world you claim that prohibited marijuana is a controlled substance. Don't be a chowderhead. *Alcohol* is a controlled substance because it is sold at regulated establishments to adults only, whereas marijuana is most certainly *not* controlled and consequently is available everywhere. An anything-goes underground economy isn't control. That's anarchy. What is prohibition? Total deregulation. This is why it is paramount that we rope in *all* illegal recreational substances as a way to keep a lawful eye over them, to make sure they don't get up to any mischief in violent, underground hands. But, you argue, cocaine and heroin are not harmless substances. That is true—and it is *precisely* the reason why these substances need to be regulated and (re)legalized. As things stand now, deaths incurred by recreational drug use occur for one of three reasons: accident, misuse, and impure product. Drug regulation is about doing the best job we can to prevent the first, avoid the second, and to completely eliminate the third. In a nutshell, there's legalization.

You worry that legalized drugs might turn us into a "nation of zombies" while forgetting that most of us (not me!) are already zombies after a fashion from ingesting one pharmaceutical drug or another at any given time, morning, noon, and night. Make no question about it, we are a drug-addled culture: antacids, Prozac, Ritalin, Zantac, Zyrtec, Zoloft, the list really can go on. Some people are depressed because they are forced off the treadmill of work, way more are stressed for being *on* the treadmill of hypercapitalism, and some people, get this, take a drug because they have a hard time moving their bowels. For criminy's sake, people don't need a stool softener to take a good shit; they need to *eat better.*

So, yes, to use a favorite cliché of yours, we do indeed have an "insatiable demand" for all sorts of drugs—and that includes you, sir. How do I know this? Oh, it's because you once said, in one of your older op-eds, that a discussion of legalization is best reserved as "idle chitchat amidst the tinkling of cocktail glasses." That's swell. You sip Ketel One among fellow liquid-drug sippers at fancy get-togethers, and I'm a criminal for inhaling a plant in the privacy of my own home. Thanks a lot. But what *would* a world that transformed idle chitchat into public policy look like? Heaven on earth, that's what.

Let's start with cocaine. Remarketing Coca-Cola in its *true* original formula is probably out of the question. The idea has great appeal but I suspect this would be difficult to pull off, marketing-wise, seeing that Coca-Cola is now a recreational drink that appeals to all age groups. There's no way the company could get away with issuing a cocaine-infused cola, not even under some "classics" adults-only banner. Coca tea, however, would work. Perhaps a diluted coca extract, a tincture, could be made available for putting into drinks. And there's no reason why the sensational coca/lime combo enjoyed by Andrew Weil can't be replicated in gum form (you'll remember my shoutout to Wrigley). Powdered cocaine, as a behind-the-counter product for adults who show identification, would be legal with explicit warnings indicating the harm that may result from compulsive use.

Heroin? A news item tells us that "twelve people died and more than one hundred addicts were treated for overdoses when heroin laced with fentanyl, a potent tranquilizer, was sold in the South Bronx." Or this, from you: "People overdose on heroin very easily. People overdose on one bag. The ingredients are not printed on the bag. It's mixed with all kinds of poisons and people die all the time." Exactly. But if heroin were legal, overdose and deaths caused by *impure* heroin would decline—no, I take that back—would disappear because, well, let's haul out the analogy once again: apart from some backwoods eccentric who likes to distill his own hooch, what alcohol user would turn to potentially impure alcohol when he can buy a quality-controlled supply whose purity is guaranteed by law?

You tell me that chronic heroin users need help. That may be so but I fail to see how prohibition facilitates such help. Not only do users have to contend with impure heroin and dirty, shared needles, they are reluctant to come forward for counseling because of laws that might get them a stint in prison. So of *course* heroin should be legal, and for three reasons (outside of putting an end to drug gangs): first, *pure* heroin, despite its dangers, is *less* dangerous than the stuff on the streets; second, users can have the freedom to seek counseling and medical assistance *if they choose to do so* without fear of arrest; and third, we'd put an end to the sharing of needles, which contribute to the spread of infectious diseases.

"But these people shouldn't be using heroin anyway." Who are you to say what people may or may not ingest? Remember our friend who said he liked opiates? I want that guy to have access to legal, top-quality heroin, not the shit he would get from some alleyway dealer. In my ideal world adults would simply purchase any opiate they so desired. But in the interim I would grudgingly condescend to a paternalistic scheme whereby physicians would distribute heroin to registered heroin users. Yes, it would be a heroin handout—but only for the hardest of long-term users. This approach would mirror what Denmark began doing in early 2010, making it the sixth country in the world to employ such a sane, sensible, and caring policy. Oh, and these clinics would come complete with injection rooms and *non*-compulsory counseling services.

I can see your eyes widening. You're appalled. You say of the British experiment from many years ago to distribute heroin "worked satisfactorily as long as addicts were few in number and all registered: five hundred a year between 1930 and 1960. It became unmanageable after 1960, when heroin had to be dispensed to more than one thousand users of the drug." But why would the dispensing of heroin to one thousand users be unmanageable when dispensing to five hundred users was manageable? It's verbal magic. As for reality, if we were to dispense heroin to only one thousand users (or even five thousand users), this country, even correcting for population size between Britain and the United States, would be in a state of bliss—and it's a state that can't come soon enough.

TURNING NOW TO marijuana, what would a liberalization of the drug laws look like? Advocates for marijuana decriminalization want to relax the laws for possession. The penalties, they say, wouldn't be as severe. Instead of a jail sentence and a criminal record you'd only get a fine. But why should the mere use of marijuana get a person a fine in the first place? As the folks at NORML like to put it, pot smokers aren't "nonviolent drug offenders"; they're marijuana consumers.

There are several states—and countries: The Netherlands, Czech Republic, Mexico—where personal possession of illegal drugs is no longer a criminal offense. Consider Portugal. After instituting a new policy on July 1, 2001, that decriminalized the possession of small amounts of marijuana and other drugs, the country has seen lower rates of chronic use, but because the *trade* in illicit drugs remains so does much of the violence associated with it (because decriminalization doesn't do anything to put modern-day Al Capones out of business). So if *users* happen to be caught, they have to appear in front of a court within three days, have the case suspended and be placed on probation or get sent to a clinic for "rehabilitation." It's regrettable that no enlightened judge will say, "Screw this nonsense. This is just dried plant matter. Do what you will with it so long as no one else gets harmed. Please leave my chambers."

And then there's entrapment, a common "side effect" of decriminalization. For a really sinister example, consider the five boroughs that make up New York City wherein marijuana possession was decriminalized in 1977. Between 1997 and 2009 approximately four hundred and seventy thousand arrests were made for marijuana possession, and in 2010 alone approximately fifty thousand people were arrested, thereby making New York City, in the eyes of many, "The Marijuana Arrest Capitol of the World." Let's look at how this appellation came to be.

Possession of marijuana on your person in NYC is subject to a traffic ticket, like a fine for being double-parked. Note the distinction: smoking weed in public or displaying a bag of weed in public is a crime, but mere possession in your pants pocket is subject to a fine. This leads to an obvious question: if a person has a dime bag in his pants pocket, how would a police officer know that? The answer is an illegal stop-and-frisk. If a person under the threatening inquisition of a police officer doesn't know to say "I do not consent to this search" and instead brings that bag of weed or joint out of his pocket, the accused will find that he has unwittingly played into the cop's hands. What was once hidden and a ticketable offense (the marijuana in the pocket) is now a crime, because the pot is now out in the open in the bright glare of a cop's view, and then the next thing that comes out after the marijuana are handcuffs. A favorite cliché comes to mind here: "vested interest." In other words, it behooves law enforcement to keep the war on marijuana users going because it helps feed the coffers—and when "crime" statistics are raised this can lead to additional federal funding. Or as Randy Barnett, a law professor at Georgetown University Law Center, puts it: "Drug law users ignore the cost of prohibition because of their 'economic dependence' on drug laws; these people profit financially from drug laws and are unwilling to undergo the economic 'withdrawal' that would be caused by their repeal."

Make no question about it: the criminalization of marijuana is a financial boon for police departments, especially with shift-ending arrests known as "collars for dollars." I will let *Urban Dictionary* define that term for you: "When a cop makes a proactive arrest minutes before his shift is over so that the paperwork and booking procedures allow for a couple hours of overtime for that officer." The degree to which we have fallen is staggering to consider: from the Founding Fathers who envisioned a hemp-based agrarian society to NYC police officers playing gotcha over a mere joint with punishing consequences. In the words of Richard Gottfried, who crafted the 1977 decriminalization law, "If that's not the police creating crime, I don't know what is."

But good luck to Portugal. I support the country's decision to move toward sane(r) drug policies. But it will only be a matter of time before the Portuguese authorities realize that most marijuana smokers are like most alcohol drinkers: responsible individuals for whom no arrest is needed for a violent act or a disturbance of the peace that did not occur. When this realization comes (it's just common sense kicking in), it will slam them like a bolt from the blue: decriminalization is nothing but an audition for full-scale legalization, where marijuana is brought back into the marketplace and sold alongside other competing goods and services—and with rules and laws in place that essentially mirror what we have for the sale and use of alcohol.

As for *your* take on legalization, listen to how nutty you sound: "The legalization proponents' message is that drug use is here to stay, constituting a civil right." That, my friend, is way fucked up. It's not a civil right *because* marijuana use is here to stay (and, yes, marijuana is here to stay); it's *inherently* a civil right because what a person puts in his body is nobody else's business—until that right interferes with another person's right to go about his day in peace.*

But you worry that legalization endorses marijuana. Let me remind your hyperventilating self as calmly as I can that the end of alcohol prohibition was not regarded as a renewed, government-directed "permission"

---

*You prohibitionists love to point out that the right to use cannabis is nowhere to be found in the Constitution. I'll let Russ Belville take care of this one: "The only reason the right to plant seeds, harvest crops, and ingest herbs wasn't placed in the Constitution is that even the best educated hemp farmers couldn't envision a time when it would be necessary to enumerate that right."
http://stash.norml.org/drug-czar-medical-marijuana-a-gateway-for-legalization

to buy and sell liquor; it was regarded as a victory for freedom and liberty. True, the government issues dietary guidelines, which function as an endorsement of how we ought to eat. But when it comes to recreational drugs the government doesn't endorse alcohol and it won't endorse marijuana. Even better, tobacco: it's legal but by no means does the government endorse it.

You go on to say that legalizing marijuana is a terrible idea because "the last thing we need to do is legitimize one more thing which is already responsible for sending more users to drug rehab than any other drug." This is straight out of Monty Python. First, brand peaceful marijuana smokers as being worthy of arrest and then with an accompanying court order frogmarch these harmless stoners into "rehabilitation" centers—and then proudly cite your self-made statistic about the "skyrocketing number" of potheads in "need" of rehabilitation. Brilliant. John Cleese will wish he had thought of this.* What's funnier is that drug court sentences actually *increase* the availability of drugs. Think about it. Some

*Though you already have: "Nationwide there are more than two thousand drug courts pushing low-level offenders to get treatment when drug use brings them into the criminal justice system." "Drug Legalization Isn't the Answer," J. Walters, *The Wall Street Journal*, March 6, 2009.

twenty-one-year-old gets arrested and is subsequently sent to a "rehabilitation" group where he meets fellow drug users and makes connections. Excellent: once the court-appointed process is over, our friend, snickering as he heads for the exit, will have acquired new contacts. Sort of like a "sexa-holic" who scores a quick hookup at group meeting.

You chirp that legalized marijuana will "legitimize its use in [our children's] eyes." That is absolutely correct. We do want to legitimize pot's use—for *adults*, in the exact same way alcohol has been legitimized.* That's the whole point. Legal marijuana is not going to be sold like easy beer that you pull out of a supermarket cooler. It will be sold in a manner akin to the way so-called "hard" liquor is sold—to adults. Nevertheless, you bemoan that legalization "will make marijuana more freely available to our children" and that legalization will create opportunities and places for teenagers to buy and sell marijuana. But these places already exist. They're called high schools. Time and again, government surveys tell us that it's

*Funny thing, though, about legitimization: we ban tobacco ads within a thousand-foot radius of high schools, but in New York City, where kids and teenagers have been known to take underground transportation, no one clamors to have rum and scotch ads removed from subway cars. What's that all about?

generally much easier for kids to get marijuana than it is to get alcohol. Once again I have to spell things out to you: alcohol is *legal* and therefore rigorously controlled and consequently hard to buy—for teenagers. Ask yourself: when's the last time you saw a gaggle of sixteen-year-olds perusing the shelves at a liquor store? Never. So I'm *really* getting tired of this failed, what-about-the-children Jedi mind trick of yours. Drop it already—and the following story gives you an excellent reason to do so.

You may not follow every kerfuffle that comes clattering in over your Teletype machine, but relevant to this discussion about teenagers is a news item you ought to know about. In early 2009 Julie Myerson, a journalist in England, published a book about her "cannabis-addicted" son. This caused quite a furor, with charges leveled at the mother that writing about her son's apparent misadventure with weed possibly jeopardized his future. But some people were supportive. One commentator came away with the impression that "Jake is a monstrous, selfish, bullying presence, a normal teenage solipsism amplified to the nth degree by skunk's powerful chemistry."

It's true that a seventeen-year-old ought not to be smoking pot. But what is Jake's side of the story? Probably that of an amotivated, strung-out loser, right? Let's check it out. Here's Jake at age twenty, in early 2009:

> "I think my parents thought that if they could break me, I'd come back to them crawling and beg to be sent to rehab. These American drugs counselors, who thrive on fear and naivety, which my parents have in bucket loads, believe that a drug addict has to hit rock bottom before they can be helped. I have spent the past three years distancing myself from them, because I look at what I like about myself and what other people like about me and it has nothing to do with them. I have survived on my own for three years, found a place to live, got myself through two university courses, played at numerous musical events: so how can I be a drug addict with no motivation and lost in life? It just doesn't add up. … My mother would say [I'm a drug addict], but I would say that I am definitely not. It's the same difference between wanting to have a drink every day and being an alcoholic. I just like smoking cannabis. Today, my drug use is frequent and enjoyable."

I know what you're thinking. "Jake is headed for trouble. He uses marijuana now; he'll be using heroin later." Ah, yes, this is just another variant of your dreaded "slippery slope": the "gateway drug" theory. Consider the Institute of Medicine, which, in case you don't know, was chartered by the National

Academy of Sciences in 1970 and serves as an advisor to the federal government. Keep that in mind: *advisor to the federal government.*

This is what the Institute has to say about your gateway theory: "[B]ecause underage smoking and alcohol use typically precede marijuana use, marijuana is not the most common, and is rarely the first, 'gateway' to illicit drug use. There is no conclusive evidence that the drug effects of marijuana are causally linked to the subsequent abuse of other illicit drugs" and "it does not appear to be a gateway drug to the extent that it is the cause or even that it is the most significant predictor of serious drug abuse; that is, care must be taken not to attribute cause to association." You should also take note of Barry Cooper, a former narcotics officer and now a vehement antiprohibitionist, and Willie Nelson. Both men have said in so many words that they were heavy drinkers but now attest to how a safer recreational drug, marijuana, has turned their lives around. Yes, marijuana is quite likely a gateway drug—*away* from so-called "harder" drugs, like alcohol.

HIGH DRIVING. Here you are with your buddies in a recent group op-ed: "Because marijuana negatively affects drivers' judgment, motor skills, and reaction time, it stands to reason that legalizing marijuana would lead to more accidents and fatalities involving drivers under its influence."

I agree that it's not a good idea to be under the influence of any psychoactive drug while driving, but when it comes to marijuana you have little to worry about: driving while high is *such* a buzz kill—which is to say that pot smokers don't like being high when they have to drive. But if someone *has* smoked pot early one evening and then later has to get behind the wheel of a car, well, most people with experience will tell you for sure that if eight or even nine pm was the last time you hit the bowl, you can totally drive home safely at eleven pm.

I'm sorry if you just soiled yourself, but if marijuana is such a killer on the roads, where are the bodies? The White House Office of National Drug Control Policy tells us that 1979 was *the* peak year for marijuana use in this country—and yet there was no vehicular holocaust on our nation's highways. Huh, what a mystery. Well, not really. A study called "Marijuana and Actual Driving Performance" from—and I must italicize here—the *United States Department of Transportation* reveals a rather blasé concern over marijuana:

> Profound drug impairment constituting an obvious traffic safety hazard could as easily be demonstrated in a laboratory performance test as anywhere else. ***But THC is not a profoundly impairing drug.*** [I've bolded this sentence to make sure you don't glide over this shocking admission from the government.] It does affect automatic information processing, even after low doses, but not to any great extent after high doses. It apparently affects controlled information processing in a variety of laboratory tests, but not to the extent [that] is beyond the individual's ability to control when he is motivated and permitted to do so in real driving.

That's great news: being high on marijuana use is of little concern to the organization that oversees the safe operation of multi-ton vehicles on our highways and rails.

Look, in order to understand *why* marijuana is not a threat, you need to understand something about alcohol. Drunkenness disengages us from our environment for the plain reason that certain aspects of our physiology, such as seeing and walking—and coordinating the movement of a motorized vehicle—are compromised by alcohol's influence on our central nervous system. Marijuana? There just isn't anything comparable. Hey, you don't have to trust me on this. Trust the folks at the Department of Neuropsychology and Psychopharmacology at Maastricht University. They conducted a study on marijuana's impairment potential on psychomotor skills and came up with some interesting results. Here you go, with my italics for emphasis:

> Alcohol significantly impaired critical tracking, divided attention, and stop-signal performance. *THC generally did not affect task performance.* However, combined effects of THC and alcohol on divided attention were bigger than those by alcohol alone. In conclusion, the present study generally confirms that heavy cannabis users develop tolerance to the impairing effects of THC on neurocognitive task performance. Yet, heavy cannabis users did not develop cross-tolerance to the impairing effects of alcohol, and the presence of the latter even selectively potentiated THC effects on measures of divided attention.

Russ Belville, piling on, tells us that "people who use cannabis consistently develop a tolerance to the psychoactive effects and are as capable as most people using other prescription medications. The FDA-approved cannabinoid prescription, Marinol (100% potent THC), has the following warning: 'Do not drive a car or operate machinery until you know how Marinol capsules affect you.' Which tells me that once you do know how Marinol effects you, go right ahead and drive. So if that's the warning for 100% pure THC, why again are we supposed to fear the 10%–20% THC cannabis user on the road?" That's fantastic. The government is telling us they are not particularly concerned by the prospect of drivers who have ingested synthetic THC—which, in turn, means they also ought not to be concerned by drivers who have ingested natural THC.

A study conducted by Britain's Transport Research Laboratory found two important things. One, while high drivers had a hard time maintaining constant speed (the research was done at a figure-eight loop) their reaction time remained unimpaired. Two, all the subjects were hyperconscious of their compromised state and so as a consequence they tended to drive with greater caution. None of this surprises me. Keep in mind what I said a moment ago about the compromised central nervous system: a drunk driver is an erratic driver with blurry vision—and a person who has lost motor control, in both senses of the term. A high driver, while certainly compromised at some level, simply isn't the dysfunctional driver that the drunk driver is.

Toronto's Centre for Addiction and Mental Health discovered the same thing: impaired (high) drivers *know* they are impaired and try to compensate—and can because impairment is simply not on par with seeing-double drunk drivers. So if you have to be driven home by a high driver or a drunk driver, hands down, you always want to go with the high driver. Yep, take the ride home with the guy at Hempfest; steer clear of the Mardi Gras reveler who says, with typical short-circuited braggadocio, c'mon, hop in, I can drive, no problem. Carl Sagan comes to mind here: "I don't advocate driving when high on cannabis, but I can tell you from personal experience that it certainly can be done. ... I have on a few occasions been forced to drive in heavy traffic when high. I've negotiated it with no difficulty at all, though I did have some thoughts about the marvelous cherry-red color of traffic lights."

In sum, this fear of pot smokers killing us all on the highways is nothing more than a lame retooling of the warnings from the 1930s and the tales, all of them tall, of knife-wielding maniacs. Wake up and the smell the java. Your morning news is here. If marijuana were a danger to society, the devastation you imagine occurring on our streets, buses, and planes *would already be happening right now*. After all, look at California and those other states that have legalized marijuana for medical use. I don't seem to be hearing stories of car pile-ups streaming out of those locales. Translation: nothing much will change after legalization except for the fact that marijuana smokers will no longer be prosecuted for breaking a law whose ethical basis is rooted in the fourteenth century.

YOU'LL REMEMBER the aftermath of Prohibition: some states became "wet" while others stayed "dry"; some states opted for government run stores while others sold alcohol for a profit—and all this occurred because at the *federal* level alcohol prohibition came to an end. We can expect to see a similar scenario play out for marijuana. One intriguing suggestion is to simply return the plant to its "primitive" state as a weed that can grow by the side of the road that's free for the taking to anyone who wants it—and then proceed accordingly: have laws in place to govern its proper use, and if people want to grow the plant privately and trade its fruit with a next-door neighbor or sell it at a farmer's market, fine. A home-grown string beans analogy is appealing, but given that many people don't want to grow marijuana just as many people don't want to grow string beans, it's obvious that legal marijuana will be just another item for sale among other goods and services in the marketplace.

Keep in mind we're not talking Wild West capitalism here. It'll be a highly regulated product. Generally speaking, the current model we have for selling alcohol is the ideal model for selling cannabis. You'd think the corollary would be tobacco. True, many tobacco smokers are passionately loyal to specific brands, but all of them are quite satisfied to get their hands on whatever pack of cancer sticks they can find. Marijuana smokers on the other hand are far more discriminating (though of course in this damn underground market we'll take what we can get). When experienced smokers speak aesthetically of marijuana they sound like passionate wine lovers who note the differences between Italian wines and French wines and merlot versus cabernet, good years versus bad. We discuss Indica versus Sativa, equatorial versus North American, mind highs versus body highs, the sweet smell of good strains, different colors, different tastes, different strengths of marijuana for different uses—and, yes, for different pleasurable mental effects as well. Speaking of which, one of the funnier scare tactics from you and other prohibitionists is this silly alarm you all have over potency. "Why would a marijuana abuser [sic] opt for a less potent drug when stronger variations are available?" Hey, I don't see you up in arms over vodka, which is stronger than beer—or over gin, which is stronger than wine. When faced with a potent strain, marijuana users do what they've always done: they smoke less of it to get the desired effect. Potency is a nonissue.

EARLY IN his administration President Obama provoked a town hall audience into laughter with his dismissive chuckle in response to a question about marijuana legalization in which he replied that it would not be a good way to "grow the economy." He is grossly mistaken. What is marijuana good for? Here you go: food, clothing, and shelter. Cannabis is *the* major organic wonder of the world, and yet you view this wonderful plant as crabgrass on the lawn of life. But let's be real. The legalization of marijuana won't be cupcakes and roses for everyone. Let's dispense with the bad news.

First, you don't have to be a genius to see that the prison industry is going to get hurt. Look at California. With close to one hundred and seventy-five thousand people in jail in a business that's booming—yes, a business: the California Department of Corrections budget was $923 million in 1985 but $5.7 billion in 2004—we'll certainly see some pushback from the prison industry. But let's make no mistake about it. At pot's relegalization, the prison industry's coffers *will* decline. George H. W. Bush once spoke of the need to build new prisons. Yeah? I say we turn these prisons into grow rooms.

The pharmaceutical industry. Dr. Tod Mikuriya estimated that the industry stands to lose about ten to twenty percent of its business to marijuana. That sounds about right. Donald Abrams, chief of oncology at San Francisco General Hospital, pretty much sums up what's likely to transpire. "I see patients who have loss of appetite, nausea from chemotherapy, pain, depression, anxiety, insomnia, and I know I have one medicine I can recommend that takes care of all these symptoms." Yeah, being able to *grow* your own medicine is going to be a real bitch for pharmaceutical execs. There's nothing they can do. It is what it is. Sales of sleep aids *will* drop when people realize they can have just a toke or two of an organic herb. Hey, you may want to short your favorite pharmaceutical stock. That sucker's going *down*.

The urinalysis industry. I have no quarrel with those who study urine for medical or research purposes. But I do have a quarrel with the arm of the industry that serves to intrude on a basic civil liberty like, oh I don't know, ownership of the organism that is me.

I don't know where I got this silly idea that the government doesn't own my body, but there it is.

But ask yourself: who cares if Tom has downed a beer or if Dick has snorted a line or if has Harry smoked a bowl—or if Lucy took a tab of LSD? What matters is not what a prospective employee may have ingested in the few days prior to an interview (or weeks or even months in the case of hair testing for marijuana), but whether or not the individual is qualified for the job and is a good fit for your team. Look, if a driver is suspected of being drunk, sure, pull him over to the side of the road and give him all the sobriety tests you want.* But as for drug testing as a requirement for employment, I look forward to seeing this $750 million market come to an end.

Finally, the liquor business stands to get smacked a little bit, and the people who work in this industry know it—and look on with alarm at the marijuana legalization movement. True, the pleasures of beer with pizza

---

*You know what else? I say we put into place an all-encompassing law that would prohibit driving under the influence of whatever drug *and* driving while tired, texting, putting on makeup, getting fellated or any number of stupid things people do behind the wheel (correction: getting fellated isn't stupid; just save that activity for later). In other words, the law would be drug-neutral: we won't care about what drug you might (or might not) be on; when pulled over to the side of the road we only want to know if you're *impaired*.

and wine with dinner are not to be denied, but at the end of the day many users of alcohol and weed have made their preference clear: given a choice they'd rather light up a joint than wind down with booze.

TURNING NOW to some good news for industry, the first order of business is to get rid of that crazy law stating that hemp products must be made from hemp that grows outside the country (Canada, mostly). Consider by analogy just how nuts this current law is. It's like saying the gallon of milk you buy every week has to come from cows that live in Europe. What a crazy world.

But can you imagine what the country might be like today if the 1942 United States government film, *Hemp for Victory*, led to a post-war initiative for hemp-based businesses that would have transformed the clothing, paper, and plastics industries?

First of all, hemp is an environmentally friendly plant. Unlike the cotton plant, cannabis is one of the most sustainable crops for industrial purposes because it doesn't need herbicides, pesticides, or fertilizers. Its fiber, the longest of all plants—I'm speaking here of Sativa, which has been known to grow as high as twenty feet (whereas Indica is rather short and squat)—is strong and durable and can be used for all sorts of applications, commercial or business.

As for the timber industry, paper made from wood will always be around, but nobody is going to miss deforestation. Remember, cannabis grows much faster than trees: marijuana seeds can rocket toward maturity in just a few weeks or months. Think about it. The infrastructure—the machinery and general processes by which large amounts of plant matter (in this case, trees) are harvested and turned into various paper commodities—is already in place and so there's no reason why the industry can't transform itself. "We used to cut down trees to make a living. Now we manage large-scale cannabis farms." No biggie.

You'd think that the oil-based plastic industry would collapse upon legalization. Again, it's a matter of adaptation. As with the infrastructure of a timber business switching to hemp, the plastics industry has the infrastructure to switch over to hemp plastic. Think of the money to be made from a wide variety of consumer products: sandwich bags, water bottles, car parts, and computer shells. I do not exaggerate: any plastic item you can think of made from petroleum—and that includes nearly all consumer and business products—can be made from plastic derived from hemp.

The carpet/clothing/fabric industry. This is yet another case of an industry simply needing to switch gears and become friends with the most durable fiber in the world. Hemp isn't a threat; it's an opportunity.

And then we have the tobacco industry. This one is easy to call. The industry would like nothing better than to redeem itself in the eyes of the public—and selling legal marijuana is the way to do it. Urban myth has it that the leading tobacco companies are ready to roll marijuana joints and get them out to the public in a matter of mere weeks after the fall of marijuana prohibition. I wouldn't be surprised. They certainly have the infrastructure to do it.

Lastly, on the food front, hemp seeds are as healthful in their own way with their own specific characteristics as are pumpkin seeds or sunflower seeds. Spooky: the balance of essential oils in the plant—linoleic and linolenic acids—perfectly matches human need. And while eating seeds is one great thing, don't forget that cannabis can also be used to make cooking oil. As for the buds of the plant, they'll most certainly be used in food, such as confectionary products—for adults only, of course. You may think this is ridiculous because, drawing an analogy to Coca-Cola, the candy bar industry is one that appeals to all ages. Fair point. But you can't forget the medical component here. Some people who are ill and want cannabis simply don't like to smoke or vaporize. They'd prefer to eat cannabis when it's mixed into a brownie or cookie. So this is a market that must and will be catered to in a fully legalized scenario.

All told, legalization is simply a transfer of economic power from the law-enforcement/prison-industry complex and the underground economy that recently rescued the global financial system (so says UN drug czar Antonio Maria Costa*) to businesses that make 100%-biodegradable fiberboard, carpets, clothing, oil, paper, plastic, and soap. And let's not forget the most obvious business of all: selling marijuana to peaceful, responsible adults who just want to get high—or to seek relief from whatever may ail them. What's more, in a world that finally came to its senses, cannabis would become one of the hottest commodities all across the globe. This includes Afghanistan, whose cli-

*"In many instances, drug money is currently the only liquid investment capital. In the second half of 2008, liquidity was the banking system's main problem and hence liquid capital became an important factor."
http://www.reuters.com/article/idUSLP65079620090125

mate makes for a perfect open-air grow house. Imagine an Afghanistan that took pride in growing and selling cannabis to a world that desires it. Instead of existing as a hot spot for war, Afghanistan would become a hot spot for pot.

And in a competitive, worldwide market, connoisseurs of topnotch bud in London or Madrid will appreciate marijuana that hails from the American Southwest much as oenophiles in Seattle and Boston enjoy Italian and French wine. Right? Take a look at the American wine industry. Napa Valley thrives quite well despite Italy and France, two of the biggest wine-producing countries in the world. Also, let's not forget that legal alcohol permits a wide range of prices and qualities, from the cheapest like Night Train to the most expensive mass-produced items like Dom Perignon. Yep, the world of buying, selling, and using legal marijuana will basically mirror the one we have for buying, selling, and using fermented berries and distilled spirits. I can't think of a better way to put it.

WHAT DOES the future hold? Well, for starters, we first have to contend with the gigglers—and I'm speaking of people who presumably have never taken a hit of weed. These are the commentators in the media who, with a veiled tone of sarcasm and mock disbelief, can't tell a straight news story about a new marijuana dispensary without closing the report with some pretend giggles and a cheesy aside along the lines of "How *crazy*! What *will* people think of next!"

There's former CNN anchor Rick Sanchez chuckling over the idea of legalizing marijuana for medical use (pot brownies for ill people who don't want to smoke are, in his words, "the last thing anybody would want at this point"). There's that Fox clown, Glenn Beck, using some pot-infused confectionary products as a prop to ridicule legalizers thereby neatly canceling out his self-made assertion that he's a libertarian.* Listen to those radio show hosts laugh at Lewis Black's suggestion that marijuana should be legalized.

The unfunny thing about all this is that I don't seem to be hearing any mirth emanating from nonviolent marijuana consumers who have been sent to jail or who have experienced asset forfeiture—boats and cars have been impounded because of a single joint—or have lost student aid or have been denied food stamps or have been kicked out of subsidized housing, and all because of

---

*Think conservatives stand for small, leave-me-alone government? Think again. Click on this address to see what Rachel Maddow serves up: http://www.msnbc.msn.com/id/26315908/#42331193

some buds from a certain plant were found on their person.*

As for elected officials and public servants, the times they are a-changin.' In 1987 Douglas Ginsburg was denied a seat on the Supreme Court because of his pot-smoking history as a college student and—horrors!—when he was an Assistant Professor at Harvard University, and yet today we have a president who said that he did inhale because "that's the point." In 1987 there were zero states legally allowing marijuana for medical use; today there are more than a dozen. I'd consider this progress.

And then there's Representative Dana Rohrabacher from California: "If it was a vote—a blind vote where nobody knew who was voting—you would have overwhelming support for legalizing marijuana out there, but they will never vote for it because they are afraid of taking on a controversial issue." Representative Jared Polis from Colorado chimed in: "I find that a lot of members of Congress privately agree that we need to change our drug policy. They're just still too timid or scared to come public with it." Well, timidity is only a part of the story. It's also

---

*In addition to reduced law-enforcement costs at prohibition's retirement, people will no longer have the economic damage associated with criminal records (this is hard to measure, but the benefits to society have got to be huge).

that the drug czar is duty bound to uphold *lies*—yes, as in the brazen and naked kind.

No, this is not some conspiracy that I know you *so* want to use against the "loony left." The head of the Office of National Drug Control Policy, who is colloquially known as the drug czar, is statutorily *required* to oppose any support of legalization in any way and to ignore any evidence that comes along and contradicts the prevailing prohibitionist view—which, let's face it, is just another kind of lying. If you don't believe me, take a look for yourself at the ONDCP's Reauthorization Act of 1998. Okay, fine, to save you time, here's the relevant passage:

> The Director [...] shall ensure that no Federal funds appropriated to the Office of National Drug Control Policy shall be expended for any study or contract relating to the legalization (for a medical use or any other use) of a substance listed in schedule I of section 202 of the Controlled Substances Act (21 U.S.C. 812) and take such actions as necessary to oppose any attempt to legalize the use of a substance (in any form) that: 1. is listed in schedule I of section 202 of the Controlled Substances Act (21 U.S.C. 812); and 2. has not been approved for use for medical purposes by the Food and Drug Administration.

Amazing, isn't it? That an arm of the government ostensibly looking for truth would

would look the other way when truth comes knocking? Well, no, this isn't amazing, because the ONDCP is not interested in the search for truth. They are interested in a corrupt status quo that maintains their agenda and ideology. So if the drug czar has an unequivocal fact in front of him like, oh I don't know, one that shows marijuana use has generally gone *down* overall among teens since the dawn of medical marijuana in 1996, he has to ignore this fact or lie about it. In late 2010, Gil Kerlikowske, the current drug czar, said on the *PBS NewsHour* that marijuana has no medical value. Message to Gil: liar, liar, pants on fire!

But if the Leader of the Free World were interested in speaking out against marijuana prohibition, here are the major points that would need to be covered in a speech to the nation:

- The President of the United States issues an Executive Order stating that the federal government no longer has any jurisdiction over the laws pertaining to the enforcement of marijuana prohibition. Translation: if the *states* want to keep this cockamamie war going just as some states stayed dry after alcohol prohibition ended, so be it.
- In addition, the president announces that anyone doing time on a *nonviolent* marijuana-related charge will be re-

> leased from prison. Anybody who was arrested with a joint, maybe a pound, okay maybe a few pounds in the trunk of the car, fuck it, I don't care if it's a guy who hauled in tons by boat or by plane. If anyone convicted and jailed on a pot charge had *zero connection* to a violent crime this person is to be set free, no questions asked. No unlawful possession of a weapon at the time you were arrested? See you later. No violence was committed when you simply transported some primo weed? Sayonara. All convictions for these people must be scrapped from the books—immediately and without further ado.

Now *that's* change I can believe in.

MEANWHILE, another kind of change is in the offing: tobacco prohibition. Interviewed on April 15, 1999, for a segment on *20/20*, Thomas Constantine, then head of the Drug Enforcement Administration, said "When we look down the road, I would say ten, fifteen, twenty years from now, in a gradual fashion, smoking will probably be outlawed in the United States."

Jumping back to heroin for a moment where you said it's worse than nicotine, you wrote this: "When cigarettes are temporarily unavailable, smokers don't initiate a crazed effort to find their next 'fix'. In contrast, people addicted to heroin commonly lie, cheat or steal to get money to buy more, so distressing are the symptoms of heroin withdrawal." What was that T-shirt I saw the other day? "I don't know what makes you so dumb but it's working." You want to see nicotine users go crazy for a fix? Ban tobacco tomorrow. Let's see what happens when cigarette smokers have to contend with a product-scarce, paranoia-inducing underground market.

And let's imagine what might happen if we were to ban this other habit-forming drug that, according to one researcher, "may be linked to male infertility as well as birth defects, and can even be passed through mother's milk into the nursing child." Lethal overdoses have occurred, but fortunately such cases are rare.

The National Institute of Drug Abuse confirmed that two hundred and eighty milligrams of this "widely used mind-altering drug" will produce "a mild, positive effect, including a feeling of well-being and alertness," noting too that "higher doses can produce anxiety and nervousness..." yet adding, with reassurance, that such "negative effects do not in themselves constitute serious health risks." This last remark is a bit hasty given that many users will "suffer temporary headaches, lethargy, and depression when they stop using it." Certainly, this isn't good news. Think of the havoc that would ensue if these addicts were deprived of their drug: bus and subway drivers asleep at the wheel; curt and testy vendors at every newspaper and magazine stall; all around irate and irascible sorts wherever we turned.

The news gets worse: after deliberately withholding the drug from a test group for two days, researchers discovered their subjects were "functionally impaired for a day and a half." One woman was so out of it she canceled her daughter's birthday party; another called in "sick" to her job. Most alarming of all was the person who went to his manufacturing job and "made costly errors." Dr. Roland Griffiths, one of two doctors who observed the test group, made a recommendation for those who want to quit: "taper off gradually." Easier said than done considering the widespread appeal of this drug. And not only is it widespread, this drug is legal and available for purchase by anyone, including teenagers. It's caffeine.*

---

*Excessive use of caffeine has been shown to increase the loss of calcium, thereby potentially contributing to the onset of osteoporosis in old age. Caffeine has also been linked to anxiety and respiratory ailments as well—and yet parents nationwide blithely let their kids ingest this psychoactive substance by way of soda at an average of about sixty-four gallons per year for every irritable child. Ah, so *caffeine* is the gateway drug. I knew we'd find the culprit!

Okay, so caffeine prohibition sounds far-fetched, and while tobacco prohibition hasn't been enacted (yet), wars against other defenseless plant products rage on. A quick snapshot of American history reveals various drug prohibitions, regional or national, occurring roughly in this order: opium, heroin, cocaine, alcohol, marijuana, and... khat? What the hell is khat? *The New York Times* says "khat contains cathinone, an amphetamine-like substance listed in the same [pharmacological] category as heroin." Oh boy. The authors of *Buzzed* tell us that "for centuries [khat] has been used recreationally by native peoples in Africa and the Middle East in social settings to promote conversation and improve social interactions." That's great. Now, here's the DEA on khat, which, it must be noted, is not widely known or used in North America (though try telling that to Canadian Somalis, who have been hounded for using their ancestral herb):

> Cathinone is the major psychoactive component of the plant Catha edulis (khat). The young leaves of khat are chewed for a stimulant effect. Enactment of this rule results in the placement of any material, which contains cathinone into Schedule I. When khat contains cathinone, khat is a Schedule I substance. During either the maturation or the decomposition of the plant material, cathi-

> none is converted to cathine, a Schedule IV substance. In a previously published final rule, the Administrator stated that khat will be subject to the same Schedule IV controls as cathine (see 53 FR 17459, May 17, 1988). When khat does not contain cathinone, but does contain cathine, khat is a Schedule IV substance.

So the takeaway is that khat, a naturally growing plant like any other, happens to contain a stimulant that functions as a natural chemical cousin to synthesized methamphetamine. Whoop-de-fuckin'-do. At least we have an excellent message for meth users: chew khat instead. There's your tagline. After all, why reach for synthetic meth, which is dangerous to produce anyway, when you can have the natural, real deal instead?* But what the folks at the DEA are indirectly telling us is that if khat becomes as popular as marijuana, we can expect to see a new drug war in which billions of additional dollars will be thrown down an ever-deepening black hole of corruption and violence—which means we can look forward to seeing khat gangs and khat cartels. I

---

*Which reminds me: instead of arresting people for manufacturing illicit methamphetamine you should arrest them for violating environmental and public safety laws. See the difference prohibition makes? Either we have meth that is produced safely (good luck with that) or we can have legally available khat, which grows freely and naturally from the ground. Which do you prefer?

wonder if this sort of thing goes on in the toad juice trade.

A story in *The New York Times* titled "Couple Avoid Jail in Toad Extract Case" tells us of a couple who "agreed" to attend a drug treatment program instead of going to jail for messing with some toads. According to the investigators, the toad excretion, which is procured by squeezing the toad's glands, produced a high so intense that the husband said he could "hear electrons jumping orbitals in molecules." Okay, so the experience enhanced his aptitude for metaphorical expression. But here's the fun part of the story: the accused were elementary school teachers at a nature camp. That's fantastic. I can see the *SNL* bit now: "Children, today we're not going to *dissect* a toad; we're going to do something different." But *did* the two encourage the children to get high as well or did they keep to themselves? The piece doesn't say though it seems fair to assume that if a bunch of kids at a nature camp *were* getting blasted on toad juice, the nation would have heard about it on the evening news. "The couple were also charged with possession of morphine, mescaline, LSD, the anesthetic ketamine, and less than an ounce of marijuana." If these people were caught swerving on a highway blooey from beer I could understand the outrage. But here, where's the crime? Who got hurt? Perhaps animal rights people might argue that squeezing liquid out of the backsides of toads is an instance of animal abuse; otherwise, we should let this phenomenon go its own weird way on the periphery of life.

And now I give you Dimethyltryptamine. DMT is found in nature in a wide variety of plants. It's also found in human beings. Science doesn't know exactly why the brain produces DMT. Doesn't matter. *That* the brain produces DMT is what's important here: it's been suggested that DMT is needed for dreaming. If that's the case, it doesn't make sense, as organisms producing DMT endogenously, that we'd be at war with an organism that produces exogenous DMT. As the old expression goes, it does not compute. And yet DMT is a Schedule I drug. In other words, the drug has a high level for abuse and no medical purpose—this, about a substance *that exists in our own bodies*. What, you're going to start arresting people when they have *dreams*? This sounds like a *very* bad Hollywood movie.

MITCH ROSENTHAL, founder of Phoenix House, once let slip the notion that drug users "are sort of pharmacologically cliff-hanging all the time." By equating cliff hanging with taking psychoactive drugs, Rosenthal hits upon a timeless truth: our desire to get high is innate, whether the "rush" comes from cliff hanging or from exercise (think of the runner's high)—or from ingesting a plant product. If some forms of mind-altering play incur a greater risk over others, well, so what? Bungee jumping is more dangerous than bowling. Playing football is more dangerous than playing golf. Playing golf is more dangerous—you might throw your back out on a bad swing!—than playing a game of horseshoes. Even having a heart attack during sex is possible.

I like how Mark Buechler puts it: "[P]art of the vital double-structure of many activities is the risk of frustration, failure, injury or even death, and right in the teeth of this risk, the bold, insouciant leap into the unknown." Exactly. This is who we are. We're always taking insouciant leaps into the unknown. It is how we forge on, make new discoveries, walk down new roads, meet new people, have new experiences—and yet to even *have* such experiences means we must have freedom and liberty. But you, with your strange cart-before-the-horse view of the world, place a concern for the harm that drugs might cause ahead of the freedom to

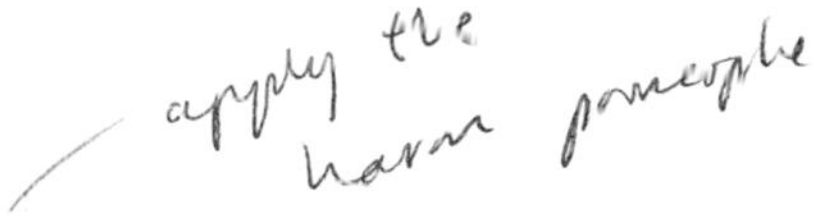

ingest them.* And why place the potential harm that might occur from using recreational drugs above the potential harms that might arise from doing other things?

Do me a favor. Go into your local hardware store and look around at all the dangerous chemicals, tools, and appliances that can be had there. Misuse of many of them can lead to severed fingers (or limbs), asphyxiation, or fatal poisoning—and yet we have the unimpeded freedom to go in that store and buy whatever we want. Wow, we can buy pesticides (vine killers), tools (hammers), and hand-held machinery (chainsaws) and use these products with care and caution, and yet you imagine societal breakdown were we to let adults, in the privacy of their own homes, smoke a bowl of benign weed now and then. Really, consider all the "hidden" pot smokers who lead peaceful lives as single people and in loving families. Go step outside your front door. Look to your left. Look to your right. Look across the street. I guarantee

---

*While we like to believe *now* that freedom and liberty are long-cherished American ideals, it's a stretch to say this country was *founded* on such ideals. Don't forget: the colonialists arrived with indentured servants—and then we had slavery. As for the Pilgrims, yes, they came to America to pursue religious freedom—and then proceeded to persecute people who had other (or no) beliefs. What does all this have to do with the drug war? It's only to say that some people who have looked at our criminal justice system have called the drug war our new Jim Crow. So what ideal, then, *was* this country founded on? Oh, that's easy: "Screw you, I got mine."

you that one of your neighbors smokes marijuana. Do you really want to go over there and arrest him? No, I didn't think so.

Returning to tobacco, yes, it's an awful fact that approximately *five million* people die every year from using this plant, but I don't ever want to see these people arrested either. I will *always* want this substance to remain legal. Yes, have stronger regulations for tobacco companies. Yes, plaster grimmer warnings on the packages. Continue to educate people about what tobacco can do to them—which appears to be working: according to the Centers for Disease Control, tobacco smoking among adults in the United States is less than half of what it was in 1965. Great—and this was achieved without putting anybody in a cage. So I don't ever want to read about search-and-seizure tobacco raids. I don't ever want to read about tobacco "traffickers" getting arrested for growing, harvesting, and transporting tobacco. I don't ever want to read about a fourteen-year-old boy getting corralled as a hit man for a tobacco cartel. So if the implications of Constantine's dystopia are not to your liking, it follows, logically, that you would withdraw your support for the prohibition of marijuana and other illegal drugs.

ON DECEMBER 20, 1819, James Madison wrote a letter to Thomas Hertell in response to receiving Hertell's pamphlet entitled "An Exposé of the causes of intemperate drinking and the means by which it may be obviated." While Madison suggests it might be ideal "if ardent spirits could be made only to give way to malt liquors," Madison notes the likely futility of enacting such a prohibition.

> A compleat suppression of every species of stimulating indulgence, if attainable at all, must be a work of peculiar difficulty, since it has to encounter not only the force of habit, but propensities in human nature. In every age and nation, some exhilarating or exciting substance seems to have been sought for, as a relief from the languor of idleness, or the fatigues of labor. In the rudest state of Society, whether in hot or cold climates, a passion for ardent spirits is in a manner universal. In the progress of refinement, beverages less intoxicating, but still of an exhilarating quality, have been more or less common. And where all these sources of excitement have been unknown, or been totally prohibited by a religious faith, substitutes have been found in opium, in the nut of the betel, the root of the Ginseng or the leaf of the Tobacco plant.

"In every age and nation, some exhilarating or exciting substance seems to have been sought for." He got that right.

You'll remember that in the Declaration of Independence the Founding Fathers spoke of our inalienable rights. The attractions of life and liberty seem obvious enough, but what exactly does the pursuit of happiness mean? Gore Vidal has called it the real joker in the deck. "No one is quite sure just what Jefferson meant, but I suppose he had it in mind that government would leave each citizen alone to develop as best he can in a tranquil climate to achieve whatever it is that his heart desires with minimum distress to other pursuers of happiness."

Might this pursuit of happiness with minimum distress also include the pursuit of altered states of mind, be it from jogging or smoking a joint? It's my guess that if Jefferson were alive today he'd be all up in your face over the drug war. Really, I see no other way to construe this joker in the deck. "If the words 'life, liberty, and the pursuit of happiness' don't include the right to experiment with your own consciousness," Terence McKenna has written, "then the Declaration of Independence isn't worth the hemp it was written on." Right. Liberty isn't perfect. Freedom is a messy thing for people who want their lives neat and ordered. Freedom can even be scary. But some form of peace is better than any kind of war.

NOTES

Page

5 **Now, you think:** T. Griesa, "There is No Case for Legalizing Drugs," *The Wall Street Journal*, August 10, 1993.

5 **You tell me how booze:** G. Will, "The Good Prohibition," *Newsweek*, June 20, 1988.

6 **An ancient Chinese burial site:** I have paraphrased Ernest Abel. See original quote at: http://www.druglibrary.org/Schaffer/hemp/history/first12000/1.htm

7 **The world's earliest known marijuana smoker:** "'Marijuana Euphoria' Comes From Within, Too, Study Says," *Newsday*, August 17, 1993.

8 **And good news for all women:** Melanie Dreher, head of the University of Iowa Nursing School, conducted a longitudinal study of Jamaican women who smoked cannabis during pregnancy. Her findings? No birth defects or behavioral problems were discovered among the children of mothers who smoked cannabis. http://patients4medicalmarijuana.wordpress.com/2009/12/20/marijuana-cannabis-use-in-pregnancy-dr-melanie-dreher/

9 **You're on record:** J. Walters, *Marijuana Inc: Inside America's Pot Industry*, MSNBC, 2009.

11 **Consider this wacky piece:** I.A. Leonard, "Peyote and the Mexican Inquisition, 1620," *American Anthropologist*, vol. 44, no. 2 (1942), p. 324-6.

12 **The inquisitor's tone:** J. Morley, "Contradictions of Cocaine Capitalism," *The Nation*, October 2, 1989.

15 **Hearst was using newsprint:** W. A. Swanberg. *Citizen Hearst*. (New York: Charles Scribner's Sons, 1961), p. 490.

16 **As the Prohibitionists demonized:** http://www.alternet.org/drugreporter/77339/

17 **I wish I could show you:** http://www.druglibrary.org/schaffer/Library/studies/vlr/vlr3.htm

17 **To get you up to speed:** http://www.drugwarrant.com/articles/why-is-marijuana-illegal/

17 **Offering accompaniment:** D. Musto, "Opium, Cocaine and Marijuana in American History, *Scientific American*, July 1991.

19 **Let's now consider:** http://www.druglibrary.net/schaffer/people/anslinger/index.htm

21 **The committee recommended:** http://www.druglibrary.org/schaffer/LIBRARY/studies/panama/panama1.htm

21 **In 1972, Consumers Union Report:** E. Brecher et al, *Consumers Union Report on Licit and Illicit Drugs* (Boston: Little, Brown and Company, 1972), p. 535.

26 **The battle [for a winnable war]:** G. Nahas, "The Decline of Drugged Nations," *The Wall Street Journal*, July 11, 1988.

26 **If we take this approach:** S. Kinzer, "German Court Allows Possession of Small Amounts of Marijuana," *The New York Times*, May 3, 1994.

27 **A lot of people:** C. Thomas, "A Reflection of Our Decadence," *The Daily News*, May 19, 1988.

27 **By this logic:** A. M. Rosenthal, "Betrayal of the Kids," *The New York Times*, August 23, 1996.

27 **The government must not:** M. A. O'Grady, "Columbia's Struggle for Law and Order," *The Wall Street Journal*, February 18, 1997.

27 **Drug dealers should be subjected:** G. Nahas, "The Decline of Drugged Nations," *The Wall Street Journal*, July 11, 1988.

28 **She said the police officers:** J. Berger, "Mother's Homemade Marijuana," *The New York Times*, October 5, 1993.

31 **These experiences:** A. Weil, *The Natural Mind* (Boston: Houghton Mifflin, 1986), p. 194.

31 **I want to be as sure of the world:** *Secrets of the Psychics*, PBS/Nova television special, 1993.

32 **When I'm high:** http://www.marijuana-uses.com/essays/002.html

34 **Consider this Reuters news item:** http://www.reuters.com/article/lifestyleMolt/idUSTRE59F0HZ20091016

34 **Apart from possible cases:** There's also been a dubious report from New Zealand citing possible cases of gum disease, dubious because neglects to factor in the poverty rates among the indigenous Maori, who are probably overrepresented in the study. Dental health care is perhaps very low, thereby leading researchers to think there may be a connection between those who smoke pot and gum disease, when instead gum disease may just be a consequence of overall poor health care. In any event, there appears to be zero clamor from dentists worldwide reporting on gum disease that can be directly linked to cannabis.

35 **Cannabinoids are a group of compounds:** Chemicals produced by the body that bind to cannabinoid receptors, but do not come from cannabis, are called endocannabinoids. These are akin to morphine receptors for which we naturally produce endorphins that fit those receptors.

36 **The problem with:** J. Millman, "Mexican Pot Gangs Infiltrates Indian Reservations in U.S.," *The Wall Street Journal*, November 5, 2009, reader comment: http://online.wsj.com/article/SB125736987377028727.html#mod%3Dtodays_us_page_one%26articleTabs%3Darticle

36 **You claim that:** E. Schlosser, "The Politics of Pot," *Rolling Stone*, March 4, 1999.

40 **I hate the term:** http://www.marieclaire.com/celebrity-lifestyle/articles/living/female-stoners

40 **I'm a middle-aged woman:** http://andrewsullivan.theatlantic.com/the_daily_dish/2009/03/the-cannabis-closet-ctd.html

41 **Okay, so a commercial pilot:** I have paraphrased Thomas Szasz: "[W]e must not forget that a commercial aircraft is not the pilot's property. It belongs to the airline company, which, together with the government, has the right to set the rules for protecting its property and the safety of the service it renders the public." T. Szasz, *Our Right to Drugs*, (Syracuse University Press, 1996), p. 162.

42 **Wal-Mart spokesman:** http://www.msnbc.msn.com/id/35913492/

42 **In states such as Michigan:** http://www.wzzm13.com/news/news_story.aspx?storyid=119421&catid=14

45 **Ronald Siegel says:** R. Siegel, *Intoxication* (New York: Pocket Books, 1990), p. 38.

45 **The stuff has a smoky, toasted-green vegetable flavor:** A. Weil, "The New Politics of Coca," *The New Yorker*, July 15, 1995.

46 **The United States:** D. Gordon, "Crack in the Penal System," *The Nation*, December 4, 1995.